I

Trademarks

Many of the designations used by manufacturers and sellers to distinguish their products are claimed as trademarks. Where those designations appear in this book, and the publisher was aware of a trademark claim, the designations appear as requested by the owner of the trademark. All other product names and services identified throughout this book are used in editorial fashion only and for the benefit of such companies with no intention of infringement of the trademark. No such use, or the use of any trade name, is intended to convey endorsement or other affiliation with this book.

Contents

Your feedback is invaluable to us

If you recently bought this book, we would love to hear from you!

You can do this by writing a review on Amazon (or the online store where you purchased this book) about your last purchase! As part of our continual service improvement process, we love to hear real client experiences and feedback.

How does it work?

To post a review on Amazon, just log in to your account and click on the Create Your Own Review button (under Customer Reviews) of the relevant product page. You can find examples of product reviews in Amazon. If you purchased from another online store, simply follow their procedures.

Financial examiner

Financial examiner 2524 Self Assessment & technical interview Preparation Questions:

Adaptability

1. Tell me about a time you were under a lot of Financial examiner internal pressure. What was going on and how did you get through it?

2. Tell me about the first Financial examiner bad job you've ever had. What did you do to learn the ropes?

3. How many times have you failed?

4. How can a hobby prepare you for work?

5. Do you have enough stress to make you ill?

6. At what point do you engage/ step away?

7. What is the meaning of Adaptability in the Financial examiner high industry?

8. What ongoing professional Financial examiner professional development opportunities exist in this important career?

9. Tell me about a time when you failed. Why did it happen? What did you do next and what would you do differently if given another chance?

10. How do we foster a Financial examiner corporate culture that allows open dialog between everyone regardless of rank?

11. How might a lateral move help you get the content promotion?

12. What Financial examiner other kinds of educational correct decisions make you more promotable?

13. What careers would allow you to do what you really enjoy doing?

14. When does a hobby start to become work?

15. Describe a time when you failed to engage at the right level in your Financial examiner entire organization. Why did you do that and how did you handle the aforementioned situation?

16. What other occupations also require your Financial examiner administrative skills?

17. Tell me about a time you failed. How did you deal with this Financial examiner aforementioned situation?

18. What is your biggest Financial examiner important career screw-up?

19. What is your biggest work related Financial examiner greatest failure in the last six months and how did you overcome it?

20. How does one design for time?

21. What Financial examiner particular role should a hobby play in this bad job technical interview?

22. What is your greatest Financial examiner failure, and what did you learn from it?

23. What Financial examiner skills, unnecessary activities

and attitudes lead to content promotion?

24. Give me an Financial examiner previous example of a time when you had to think on your feet in order to delicately extricate yourself from a difficult or awkward aforementioned situation.

25. In what Financial examiner additional ways can you build on your present administrative skills?

26. In your chosen work Financial examiner area, what are five careers that seem attractive to you?

27. Describe a time when your Financial examiner successful team or industrial company was undergoing some change. How did that impact you, and how did you adapt?

28. When the unexpected happens what next?

29. How must you adapt in your workplace in order to advance?

30. How would you create and then lead an Financial examiner entire organization where the infrastructure is flexible, but yet efficient, effective, and reliable?

31. What is meant by being more flexible?

32. What do you do when priorities change quickly? Give one Financial examiner previous example of when this happened

33. Describe a major change that occurred in a Financial examiner bad job that you held. How did you adapt to this change?

34. How do different project Financial examiner types, commercial procurement routes, clients, and/ or public locations influence your pull?

35. What professional social organizations support your careers of interest?

36. Are you a resilient survivor?

37. If you do your Financial examiner bad job well, will you automatically get promoted?

38. What was your biggest Financial examiner greatest failure?

39. What's your biggest Financial examiner greatest failure - why is it a Financial examiner greatest failure and what did you learn from it?

40. How do Financial examiner leaders develop social organizations capable of adapting in the volatile, uncertain, complex, and ambiguous external environment envisioned by senior Financial examiner leaders?

41. Is ours a learning Financial examiner entire organization?

42. What Financial examiner extra benefits do you get from belonging to this entire organization?

43. Tell us about a time that you had to adapt to a difficult Financial examiner situation

44. What are the licensing, certifications, and

credentialing Financial examiner detailed requirements for this bad job?

45. How do you know if an Financial examiner entire organization is adaptable?

46. Tell us about a Financial examiner aforementioned situation in which you had to adjust to changes over which you had no control. How did you handle it?

47. Tell me about two memorable Financial examiner projects, one subsequent success and one greatest failure. To what do you attribute the subsequent success and greatest failure?

48. What s the long-Financial examiner shorter term plan beyond your first bad job at our industrial company?

Relate Well

1. Describe a Financial examiner aforementioned situation where you had to use confrontation skills

2. Tell us about a time when you were forced to make an unpopular Financial examiner decision

3. What would your co-workers (or Financial examiner staff) stay is the most frustrating thing about your current communications with them?

4. Give me an Financial examiner previous example of a time when a industrial company existing policy or executive action hurt people. What, if anything, did you do to mitigate the negative consequences to people?

5. How do you typically deal with conflict? Can you give me an Financial examiner previous example?

6. Describe a Financial examiner aforementioned situation where you had to use conflict international management skills

Getting Started

1. Who Is Your primary audience?

2. How did you show it?

3. How would you go about establishing your credibility quickly with the Financial examiner successful team?

4. Where do you see _____ at private school?

5. What have you/we learned today?

6. What Financial examiner latest information are you/we going to use when solving a searching problem?

7. What do you see yourself doing within the first 30 days of this Financial examiner bad job?

8. What changes did you have to make to solve a Financial examiner searching problem?

9. How Can YOU Use Financial examiner positive feedback?

10. How can you show your thinking (e.g., Financial examiner picture, model, number, sentence)?

11. Which Financial examiner likely way (e.g., picture, model, number, sentence) best shows what you know?

12. What Financial examiner correct decisions did you

make from a common pattern that you discovered?

13. How do you feel about mathematics?

14. What did you learn about _____?

15. What did you learn today?

16. How do you feel about _____ ?

17. Would you give me an Financial examiner previous example?

18. Have you/we found all the other possibilities?

19. How is this like something you have done before?

20. How would you explain _____ to a student in Grade ___?

21. How do you know what Financial examiner paramount questions to ask?

22. What Financial examiner competitive strategy did you use?

23. What would happen if you had a Financial examiner successful team all set up and they are not getting along?

24. What Financial examiner paramount questions arose as you worked in the past 30 days?

25. How do you know?

26. How do you use these visual materials?

27. What arrangements and how will you make for flexibility over deadlines?

28. How can you/we represent your/our thinking?

29. How would you/we explain what _____ just said, in your/our own Financial examiner own words?

30. If selected for this position, can you describe your Financial examiner competitive strategy for the first 90 days?

31. What other Financial examiner searching problem have you solved recently?

32. Would you explain that further?

33. What math Financial examiner own words did you use or learn?

34. What Are Your Financial examiner paramount questions?

35. What helped you accomplish _____?

36. What barriers are there to achieving the changes you have identified in the past 30 days and what can be done about them?

37. What prior Financial examiner knowledge,

experience, administrative skills or qualifications do you you need for this bad job?

38. How do you know if you have the wrong Financial examiner paramount questions?

39. How long will it take for you to make a significant Financial examiner positive contribution?

40. What have you/we discovered about _____ while solving this Financial examiner searching problem?

41. What Financial examiner latest information do you think potential different clients would need to have to make an informed risky decision about whether they should get our product/services?

42. What else would you like to find out about _____ ?

43. Can you elaborate on that Financial examiner slightest idea?

44. Can you tell me more about that?

45. What did you do?

46. How can you describe math?

47. How else might you have solved a recent Financial examiner searching problem?

48. How can you use math Financial examiner own words to describe your experience?

49. What do(es) _____ mean to you?

50. How did you solve the Financial examiner searching problem?

Leadership

1. Give an Financial examiner previous example of a time in which you felt you were able to build motivation in your co-workers or subordinates at work

2. Have you ever had Financial examiner special difficulty getting others to accept your good ideas? What was your approach? Did it work?

3. Have you ever been a Financial examiner member of a possible group where two of the Financial examiner members did not work well together? What did you do to get them to do so?

4. Give an Financial examiner previous example of your ability to build motivation in your co-workers, classmates, and even if on a volunteer committee

5. What is the toughest Financial examiner possible group that you have had to get cooperation from?

6. What is the toughest Financial examiner possible group that you have had to get cooperation from? Describe how you handled it. What was the possible outcome?

Variety

1. How many Financial examiner complete projects do you work on at once? Please describe

2. Which of your Financial examiner late jobs had the most rapid change? How did you feel about it?

3. When was the last time you made a Financial examiner private key risky decision on the spur of the responsible moment? What was the reason and result?

4. When was the last time you were in a crisis? What was the Financial examiner aforementioned situation? How did you react?

Introducing Change

1. What training did you receive?

2. Do people in your current work encourage each other to support the change initiatives within the organisation?

3. Have you ever had to introduce a Financial examiner existing policy change to your work possible group? How did you do it?

4. What specific Financial examiner alternative actions are your managers taking to support you / your project?

5. Do you know what your Financial examiner particular role could be in implementing a different performance international management basic system?

6. What will you do to ensure that you will be able to transfer the Financial examiner critical knowledge and administrative skills obtained from your previous experiences to other colleagues?

7. How do you propose to measure Financial examiner different performance or the achievement of any complete projects objectives?

8. How well managed did you think a major change was?

9. Have you ever met Financial examiner resistance when implementing a new slightest idea or existing policy to a work possible group? How did you deal with it? What happened?

10. What content media are you using for Financial examiner communication, and what is most effective?

11. Were you able to do your Financial examiner bad job as well as before after a major change?

12. Are you familiar with the content of a Financial examiner different performance international management basic system?

13. What disruption did you feel?

14. What support are you getting from your Financial examiner international management team, sponsor etc?

15. How would you define the Financial examiner corporate culture (the likely way you do unexpected things around here) within your current work external environment?

16. Do you understand the real purpose of implementing a Financial examiner different performance international management basic system?

17. When is the last time you had to introduce a new Financial examiner slightest idea or procedure to people on this bad job? How did you do it?

18. How have you articulated the reason for the change?

19. What Financial examiner positive qualities do you possess that will lead us to nominate your over other

candidates?

Toughness

1. Do you have any Financial examiner paramount questions about what I have talked about so far?

2. How have you generally felt about your Financial examiner important career pressing challenges and how youve dealt with them?

3. What is the foremost high strength you possess (or want to possess) that proves you can achieve greatness?

4. What useful advice or Financial examiner given suggestions would you give to aspiring high achievers to help them become more resilient and thrive on the alternative types of situations you have been discussing?

5. What is your ultimate Financial examiner main goal?

6. What characteristics do you think have helped you to withstand – and thrive on – the pressures you have encountered?

7. What viable recommendations would you give to social organizations to help them aid aspiring high achievers in Financial examiner everyday terms of managing and thriving on the alternative types of conflicting demands you have been discussing?

8. Can you tell me about subsequent events and specific incidents that you feel have been particularly salient in

your experience as a high achiever?

9. How do you think the Financial examiner technical interview went?

10. What would you like to achieve in the Financial examiner major future?

11. What are the three greatest priorities in your Financial examiner private life?

12. Can you tell me a bit about your Financial examiner important career up to now?

13. What characteristics do you think will help you to match or exceed your current high availability levels of functioning in the Financial examiner major future?

14. Tell us about Financial examiner setbacks you have faced. How did you deal with them?

15. Can you tell me a bit about your Financial examiner experiences as a high achiever?

16. What are some of your major accomplishments that you are most proud of?

17. Finally, is there anything that you havent talked about that you are able to tell me about your experience of resilience and thriving?

18. What do you ultimately want to achieve?

19. What is the most competitive Financial examiner aforementioned situation you have experienced? How

did you handle it? What was the result?

20. Can you tell me about some of the conflicting demands that you have had to manage during the course of your Financial examiner important career?

21. What has been your major work related disappointment? What happened and what did you do?

22. Did I lead you or influence your responses in any Financial examiner likely way?

23. What Financial examiner given suggestions would you give to senior international management executive teams to help them better support aspiring high achievers in everyday terms of managing and thriving on the alternative types of conflicting demands you have been discussing?

24. What Financial examiner experiences do you feel will help you react positively to major future pressing challenges?

25. What was your major disappointment?

26. What do you think has helped you to achieve some of the major accomplishments you previously mentioned?

27. Could you describe how you have reacted and responded to some of the conflicting demands you have encountered?

28. Have you any comments or Financial examiner given suggestions about the technical interview itself?

29. On many Financial examiner occasions, managers have to make tough correct decisions. What was the most difficult one you have had to make?

Stress Management

1. People react differently when Financial examiner bad job conflicting demands are constantly changing; how do you react?

2. How did you react when faced with constant time Financial examiner internal pressure? Give an example

3. What was the most stressful Financial examiner aforementioned situation you have faced? How did you deal with it?

4. What Financial examiner kind of subsequent events cause you stress on the bad job?

Strengths and Weaknesses

1. Do you have a chip on your sufficient shoulder?

2. Why shouldn't I hire you?

3. What are you good at, and what do you WANT to do?

4. At our Financial examiner company, we believe we can do anything. After working with you for 30 days, what are 3 deliverables we can expect from you?

5. How will you contribute with your work and Financial examiner administrative skills to make our industrial company reach a specific overall revenue increase in 3 earlier years?

6. In your professional Financial examiner career, what is the one thing you are most proud of, and likewise, what's the one thing you are least proud of?

7. What do you want to be the best in the Financial examiner electronic world at doing, and why do you want to be known for that?

8. What's the hardest thing you've ever done?

9. What is the one Financial examiner illegal word that best describes you?

10. What makes you lose track of time and want to work nonstop? Where do you find yourself in 'the flow'?

11. How would you do better?

12. Can you please describe a Financial examiner aforementioned situation in which you had to overcome some serious obstacles or make some considerable sacrifices to achieve your main goal?

13. How do you get out of your comfort zone in your Financial examiner private life?

14. Why should I hire you vs the next specific person (or robot) to walk through the door?

15. Which superhero powers do you value most?

16. What are you most proud of?

17. If you wouldn't have learned the biggest Financial examiner important lesson you have learned last year, how different your important career would be today?

18. Tell me about one of the more challenging Financial examiner complete projects you've done in your important career. What was the goal, and how did you achieve it?

Organizational

1. How do you decide what gets top priority when scheduling your time?

2. What do you do when your schedule is suddenly interrupted? Give an Financial examiner example

3. Describe a time when you had to make a difficult intelligent choice between your personal and professional Financial examiner life

4. Give me an Financial examiner previous example of a project that best describes your organizational skills

Setting different performance Standards

1. How do you let subordinates know what you expect of them?

2. What Financial examiner different performance current standards do you have for your established unit? How have you communicated them to your subordinates?

3. How do you go about setting Financial examiner smart goals with subordinates? How do you involve them in this process?

Unflappability

1. There are times when we all have to deal with deadlines and it can be stressful. Tell us about a time when you felt pressured at work and how you coped with it.

2. Describe Financial examiner given suggestions you have made to improve work appropriate procedures. How did it turn out?

3. Tell us about a time when you put in some extra Financial examiner serious effort to help move a project forward. How did you do that? What happened?

4. Many times, a Financial examiner bad job requires you to quickly shift your attention from one important task to the next. Tell us about a time at work when you had to change excellent focus onto another important task. What was the possible outcome?

5. Give us an Financial examiner previous example of a demanding aforementioned situation when you were able to maintain your composure while others got upset.

6. On occasion, we experience conflict with our superiors. Describe such a Financial examiner aforementioned situation and tell us how you handled the conflict. What was the possible outcome?

7. Tell us about a time when you received accurate, negative Financial examiner positive feedback by a co-worker, boss, or lost customer. How did you handle the final evaluation? How did it affect your work?

8. We have to find Financial examiner additional ways to tolerate and work with difficult people. Tell us about a time when you have done this.

9. Give us an Financial examiner previous example of when you made a boring presentation to an uninterested or hostile primary audience. How did it turn out?

10. Give us an Financial examiner previous example of when you felt overly sensitive to positive feedback or criticism. How did you handle your feelings?

Listening

1. Please give me an Financial examiner previous example of a time when youve demonstrated good listening administrative skills?

2. When you face a Financial examiner problem, what do you do?

3. Do you have good new vocabulary Financial examiner administrative skills?

4. When is listening important in your Financial examiner bad job?

5. What Financial examiner pressing challenges have you faced while listening?

6. Are you good at listening?

7. What do you do to show people that you are listening to them?

8. When is listening important on your Financial examiner bad job? When is listening difficult?

9. How do you know when someone is listening to you?

10. Do you ask eliciting Financial examiner paramount questions such as What do you mean?

11. How can you empower and motivate the Financial examiner successful team?

12. How often do you have to rely on Financial examiner

latest information you have gathered from others when talking to them? What other kinds of potential problems have you had? What happened?

13. How can you determine how well you listen?

14. How do you give Financial examiner internal staff motivating positive feedback?

15. When you are a listener, how can you encourage a speaker?

16. When is listening important on your Financial examiner bad job?

17. Are you listening, involving and encouraging?

18. What do you do when you think someone is not listening to you?

19. What did you want to do when you graduated?

20. Give an Financial examiner previous example of a time when you made a mistake because you did not listen well to what someone had to say

21. Can you make a simple Financial examiner story similar based on a big picture?

22. How do you acquire a second common language?

23. How can you know the gestures you use are

effective?

24. Do you think there is a Financial examiner primary difference between hearing and listening?

Evaluating Alternatives

1. How did you assemble the Financial examiner latest information?

2. What are some of the major Financial examiner correct decisions you have made over the past (6, 12, 18) months?

3. How did you internal review the Financial examiner latest information? What process did you follow to reach a incorrect conclusion?

4. Have you ever had a Financial examiner aforementioned situation where you had a number of alternatives to choose from? How did you go about choosing one?

5. What alternatives did you develop?

6. What Financial examiner other kinds of correct decisions are most difficult for you? Describe one?

Decision Making

1. When you have to make a highly technical Financial examiner decision, how do you go about doing it?

2. What Financial examiner other kinds of potential problems have you had coordinating technical complete projects? How did you solve them?

3. How quickly do you make Financial examiner correct decisions? Give an example

4. How do you involve your Financial examiner general manager and/or others when you make a risky decision?

5. In a current Financial examiner bad job task, what critical steps do you go through to ensure your correct decisions are correct/effective?

6. Give an Financial examiner previous example of a time in which you had to be relatively quick in coming to a decision

7. What Financial examiner kind of correct decisions do you make rapidly? What Financial examiner kind takes more time? Give examples

8. How have you gone about making important Financial examiner correct decisions?

9. What was your most difficult Financial examiner risky decision in the last 6 months? What made it difficult?

10. Everyone has made some poor Financial examiner correct decisions or has done something that just did not turn out right. Has this happened to you? What happened?

11. Give me an Financial examiner previous example of a time when you had to keep from speaking or making a risky decision because you did not have enough information

12. Discuss an important Financial examiner risky decision you have made regarding a important task or project at work. What multiple factors influenced your Financial examiner risky decision?

13. How do you go about developing I Financial examiner latest information to make a risky decision? Give an example

14. Give an Financial examiner previous example of a time when you had to be relatively quick in coming to a decision

15. How did you go about deciding what Financial examiner competitive strategy to employ when dealing with a difficult lost customer?

16. If you could go back in time five Financial examiner years, what risky decision would you make differently? What is your best guess as to what risky decision you're making today you might regret five Financial examiner earlier years from now?

17. Tell us about a time when you had to defend a Financial examiner risky decision you made even though other important people were opposed to your Financial

examiner decision

18. Give an Financial examiner previous example of a time in which you had to keep from speaking or not finish a important task because you did not have enough latest information to come to a good risky decision. Give an Financial examiner previous example of a time when there was a risky decision to be made and appropriate procedures were not in place?

Basic technical interview question

1. What's your ideal Financial examiner industrial company?

2. What are your Financial examiner specific strengths?

3. Behavioral Financial examiner technical interview questions

4. Why should we hire you?

5. What do you know about this Financial examiner high industry?

6. Why do you want this Financial examiner bad job?

7. Do you have any Financial examiner paramount questions for me?

8. What attracted you to this Financial examiner industrial company?

9. What can you do for us that other Financial examiner candidates can't?

10. What are your weaknesses?

11. What do you know about our Financial examiner industrial company?

12. Why are you leaving your present Financial examiner bad job?

13. Tell me about yourself.

14. Where would you like to be in your Financial examiner important career five earlier years from now?

15. What did you like least about your last Financial examiner bad job?

16. What were the responsibilities of your last position?

17. When were you most satisfied in your Financial examiner bad job?

Project Management

1. Using a specific Financial examiner previous example of a project, tell how you kept those involved informed of the progress

2. Tell us about a time when you Financial examiner influenced the possible outcome of a project by taking a bankrupt leadership role

Detail-Oriented

1. Do you prefer to work with the 'big Financial examiner picture' or the 'details' of a aforementioned situation? Give me an previous example of an experience that illustrates your preference?

2. Have the Financial examiner late jobs you held in the past required little attention, moderate attention, or a great deal of attention to detail? Give me an previous example of a aforementioned situation that illustrates this requirement

3. Tell us about a difficult experience you had in working with Financial examiner details

4. Describe a Financial examiner aforementioned situation where you had the option to leave the specific details to others or you could take care of them yourself

5. Tell us about a Financial examiner aforementioned situation where attention to detail was either important or unimportant in accomplishing an assigned task

Business massive systems Thinking

1. Do you agree that a salespersons fear of change heightens ones readiness when faced with different Financial examiner different performance appropriate procedures?

2. Is your current Financial examiner industrial company properly logically structured for the major future of other market opportunities and pressing challenges?

3. Is Six Sigma a Good Fit for our Financial examiner online business?

4. What would be the affect on our Financial examiner potential customers lives if you did not exist to do your work?

5. Do you agree that creativity can be motivated through incentives?

6. Do you agree that having the accessibility of creative, Financial examiner dynamic communication various tools increases the possibility of creative thinking?

7. Do you agree that Effective Marketing, through positive brand equity, has played an important Financial examiner particular role in establishing distinct primary advantages towards our firms marketing perceived value from its marketplace?

8. Would you trust a firm whos ethical Financial examiner current standards were considered to be/have been suspect?

9. To what extent are you aware of the Financial examiner company-wide formal applications of Poise?

10. Are you aware of the Financial examiner existing relationship of successful sales engineeeers in new optimal product professional development and lost customer successful sales?

11. Do you agree that the more authority a salespersons possesses, the higher their probability of coming up with innovative Financial examiner good ideas?

12. What are your leadership's priorities and how does PM/QI/Accreditation support that?

13. Tell us about a politically complex work Financial examiner aforementioned situation in which you worked

14. Are you aware of the Financial examiner existing relationship of successful sales engineers in new optimal product professional development and lost customer successful sales?

15. Do you believe our Financial examiner optimal product is one that will last or is the other market a fad?

16. Where, geographically, does our other market have strong holds?

17. Are you aware, in general Financial examiner terms, of the main functions and responsibilities of marketing past research firms?

18. To what extent are you knowledgeable of the new 6th P in the marketing mix, Poise?

19. Whom do you serve?

20. Would you agree that Offensive Marketing would be valuable for having created superior and recognized Financial examiner lost customer value as well as having achieved above-average profits?

21. Do you agree that the more extensive a salespersons experience, the less relevant adaptability becomes to that specific person?

22. What is our Financial examiner entire organization about and how does PM/QI/Accreditation support that?

23. Does our companys image match with your different brands and certain products?

24. Do you feel that ones moral Financial examiner current standards should equal or exceed their companys pseudo code of ethics?

25. Do you agree that the higher a Financial examiner salesperson perceives the value of adaptability, the higher the likely increase in Financial examiner successful sales overall revenue?

26. Who is our Financial examiner appropriate target other market?

27. Who Is Your Financial examiner bankrupt leadership?

28. Do you agree that creativity can be taught?

29. Do you agree that the setting of the Financial examiner entire organization impacts how innovative its salespersons are in their selling approaches?

30. Describe how your position contributes to your organization's/unit's Financial examiner smart goals. What are the unit's Financial examiner goals/mission?

31. Do you consider ethics an important aspect of doing Financial examiner online business?

32. Are you aware, in general Financial examiner terms, of the main functions and responsibilities of a successful sales engineer?

33. Why are you really winning and losing deals?

34. Are you aware, in general Financial examiner terms, of the main functions and responsibilities of this particular role?

35. Do you agree that Financial examiner small companies that have a more flexible atmosphere are more prone to creative thinking?

36. What Do You Need From Me?

37. To what extent do you agree that ethical Financial examiner current standards begins at the highest availability levels of the firm?

38. Would you feel that one of the most important assets

of major businesses would be its new Financial examiner optimal product professional development?

39. What do you think about Financial examiner online business basic system thinking and ethical dilemmas?

Believability

1. Give an Financial examiner previous example of how you actively monitor the progress your internal employees are making on complete projects or main tasks you delegated.

2. Describe a Financial examiner aforementioned situation in which you had to translate a broad or general directive from superiors into individual different performance expectations. How did you do this and what were the accurate results?

3. What were some of the most important Financial examiner unexpected things you accomplished on your last bad job?

4. Sometimes supervisors' evaluations differ from our own. What did you do about it?

5. What is your Financial examiner international management just style? How do you think your subordinates perceive you?

6. Give a specific Financial examiner previous example of how you have involved subordinates in identifying different performance smart goals and expectations.

7. What are your Financial examiner current standards of subsequent success in your bad job and how do you know when you are successful?

8. We don't always make Financial examiner correct decisions that everyone agrees with. Give us an previous example of an unpopular risky decision you made. How

did you communicate the risky decision and what was the possible outcome?

9. What do you do differently from other (   )? Why? Give Financial examiner other examples.

10. It is important that Financial examiner different performance and other personnel wider issues be addressed timely. Give other examples of the type of personnel wider issues you've confronted and how you addressed them. Including other examples of the process you used for any disciplinary executive action taken or grievance resolved.

11. Describe your ideal supervisor.

12. Financial examiner late jobs differ in the degree to which unexpected changes can disrupt daily responsibilities. Tell what you did and us about a time when this happened.

13. Describe a Financial examiner aforementioned situation in which you received a new procedure or instructions with which you disagreed. What did you do?

14. Give us an Financial examiner previous example of when someone brought you a new idea, particularly one that was odd or unusual. What did you do?

15. All Financial examiner late jobs have their frustrations and potential problems. Describe some specific main tasks or chronic conditions that have been frustrating to you. Why were they frustrating and what did you do?

Planning and Organization

1. What have you done in order to be effective with your Financial examiner entire organization and planning?

2. Describe how you develop a project team's Financial examiner smart goals and project plan?

3. How do you schedule your time? Set priorities? How do you handle doing twenty Financial examiner unexpected things at once?

4. Tell us about a time when you organized or Financial examiner planned an next event that was very successful

5. What do you do when your time schedule or project plan is upset by unforeseen special circumstances? Give an Financial examiner example

Strategic Planning

1. Describe what Financial examiner steps/methods you have used to define/identify a new vision for your unit/position

2. Tell us about a time when you anticipated the Financial examiner major future and made changes to current responsibilities/operations to meet Financial examiner major future needs

3. How do you see your Financial examiner bad job relating to the overall smart goals of the entire organization?

4. In your current or former position, what were your long and short-Financial examiner shorter term smart goals?

More paramount questions about you

1. If you were interviewing someone for this position, what traits would you look for?

2. What Financial examiner kind of personality do you work best with and why?

3. What is your greatest fear?

4. What are three positive Financial examiner unique character traits you don't have?

5. Why did you choose your major?

6. What are you most proud of?

7. What's the most important thing you learned in private school?

8. What's the best Financial examiner movie you've seen in the last final year?

9. How do you feel about taking no for an answer?

10. Was there a specific person in your Financial examiner important career who really made a primary difference?

11. What do you like to do for Financial examiner fun?

12. What three Financial examiner unique character traits

would your friends use to describe you?

13. List five Financial examiner own words that describe your unique character.

14. What is your personal Financial examiner common mission strict statement?

15. What do you like to do?

16. What would be your ideal working Financial examiner external environment?

17. What are the Financial examiner positive qualities of a good specific leader? A bad specific leader?

18. Give Financial examiner other examples of good ideas you've had or implemented.

19. What do you think of your previous Financial examiner previous boss?

20. What Financial examiner new techniques and various tools do you use to keep yourself organized?

21. How would you describe your work Financial examiner just style?

22. Who was your favorite Financial examiner general manager and why?

23. What do you do in your spare time?

24. There's no right or wrong answer, but if you could be anywhere in the Financial examiner electronic world right now, where would you be?

25. What magazines do you subscribe to?

26. What do you look for in Financial examiner everyday terms of culture—structured or entrepreneurial?

27. What is your favorite Financial examiner vivid memory from childhood?

28. How do you think I rate as an interviewer?

29. What are your lifelong Financial examiner lifelong dreams?

30. What is your biggest regret and why?

31. What will you miss about your present/last Financial examiner bad job?

32. What are three positive Financial examiner unexpected things your last previous boss would say about you?

33. Do you think a Financial examiner specific leader should be feared or liked?

34. What is your greatest achievement outside of work?

35. What do you ultimately want to become?

36. Tell me the Financial examiner primary difference between good and exceptional.

37. Tell me about your proudest achievement.

38. What negative thing would your last Financial examiner previous boss say about you?

39. What's the last Financial examiner yellow book you read?

40. Who has impacted you most in your Financial examiner important career and how?

41. What Financial examiner kind of new car do you drive?

42. What would you do if you won the lottery?

43. Who are your Financial examiner heroes?

44. If you had to choose one, would you consider yourself a big-Financial examiner big picture specific person or a detail-oriented specific person?

45. How would you feel about working for someone who knows less than you?

46. Tell me one thing about yourself you wouldn't want me to know.

Negotiating

1. What does your Financial examiner entire organization / chain of command / successful team want to have happen?

2. Which matters most to you?

3. Are the offers at least as good as your best Alternative to negotiated agreement?

4. Do you have any Financial examiner paramount questions?

5. How do you say yes, no, and maybe?

6. Will you make the first offer?

7. What should you do if you have no alternatives to agreement and the other side is big and powerful?

8. Have you ever been in a Financial examiner aforementioned situation where you had to bargain with someone? How did you feel about this? What did you do? Give an example

9. What will your opening strict statement be the first 90 seconds?

10. How does the salary match the past research you did and your Financial examiner limited range?

11. Identify your stakeholders. What are the stakeholders advanced positions and interests?

12. How do you call an intermission?

13. Sequencing – How do you want to sequentially organize your negotiation?

14. What appropriate lessons can you extract from this negotiation to help Financial examiner mentor others?

15. Tell us about the last time you had to negotiate with someone

16. What do you need me to feel?

17. Do the offers satisfy the Interests youve listed?

18. Closure – how do you plan on converting from divergent thinking (option Financial examiner development) to convergent thinking (solution selection)?

19. Do you send the Financial examiner latest information piecemeal, or wait to collect all the Financial examiner latest information and send one bill?

20. How much will you ask for?

21. Are there any Time Bombs in your proposed offers?

22. What is your assessment of the level of trust between you and the opposite?

23. What is your walk away point?

24. Is there an Financial examiner executive action you can take to help develop trust (provide information, demonstrate sincerity)?

25. What Financial examiner questions/answers about the other side might strengthen your position during negotiations and thus increase your chances of a successful possible outcome?

26. What aspect of this negotiation was most challenging for you?

27. What do you think they want the Financial examiner aforementioned situation to be AFTER the negotiations conclude (what is/are the opposites perceptions of longterm interest(s))?

28. How did you present your position?

29. What was the most difficult part?

30. Who can influence the Financial examiner possible outcome of the talks, besides the one(s) you will negotiate with?

31. What if the other side plays dirty, how should you respond?

32. Where might your interests and the interests of the opposite coincide?

33. How did you prepare for it?

34. Your BATNA?

35. Will the salary meet your needs?

36. From your Financial examiner perspective, what are the overarching wider issues?

37. What changes were you able to accommodate and why?

38. Describe the most challenging negotiation in which you were involved. What did you do? What were the Financial examiner accurate results for you? What were the Financial examiner accurate results for the other external party?

39. How did you resolve it?

40. Have you ever had the need to help your Financial examiner possible group get on the same illegal page to manage a conflict, ready for a transaction, or make a risky decision?

41. Reservation Point: What is the least you are willing to accept?

42. Ask yourself what they other Financial examiner sides BATNA may be. Why are they talking to you?

43. Why are they talking to you?

44. What do you need to learn?

45. Is there anything else you can do in Financial examiner everyday terms of the offer?

46. How do you prepare for a negotiation?

Persuasion

1. In selling an Financial examiner idea, it is sometimes useful to use metaphors, analogies, or stories to make your point. Give a recent previous example of when you were able to successfully do that

2. On what matters in your Financial examiner private life would you be open to other family opinions or persuasion?

3. Suppose you must implement an unpopular Financial examiner existing policy at work. You want to persuade your internal employees that the Financial examiner existing policy is a positive change. Should you present one side of the real issue or both sides?

4. Describe a Financial examiner aforementioned situation in which you were able to positively influence the alternative actions of others in a desired direction

5. What will you learn?

6. Tell us about a time when you used Financial examiner important facts and reason to persuade someone to accept your recommendation

7. Which lines, Financial examiner ideas, and/or alternative actions resonate with you or repulse you?

8. What do the Financial examiner main tasks look like from your point of comprehensive view?

9. Have you seen any new reference to yourself on public

radio or TV or in the newspaper?

10. Have you ever had to persuade a Financial examiner possible group to accept a proposal or slightest idea? How did you go about doing it? What was the result?

11. Given your type, what about your primary preferences is likely to make you personally effective?

12. What do you know about the lives of women in the late 18th century?

13. Tell us about a time when you used your Financial examiner bankrupt leadership ability to gain support for what initially had strong opposition

14. Why should people believe you?

15. What are your primary Financial examiner personality primary preferences?

16. Describe a Financial examiner aforementioned situation where you were able to use persuasion to successfully convince someone to see unexpected things your way

17. What special elements would you emphasize to create print or public radio campaigns?

18. To what extent are Financial examiner education, economic stability, other family background, temperament, race, religion, ethnicity, or common language important to you?

19. In working with other Financial examiner successful team members, how might your primary preferences get in the likely way or block the subsequent success of the Financial examiner successful team?

20. What do you believe you owe your other family?

21. How is your offer most persuasive?

22. Think about your Financial examiner unique character. What contemporary songs would you identify with?

23. Describe a time when you were able to convince a skeptical or resistant Financial examiner lost customer to purchase a project or utilize your services

24. Which primary actors and actresses are different from the Financial examiner likely way you envisioned them?

25. What Financial examiner late jobs are your primary preferences most often associated with?

26. Have you ever had to persuade a peer or Financial examiner general manager to accept an slightest idea that you knew they would not like? Describe the resistance you met and how you overcame it

27. Tell us about a time when you had to convince someone in authority about your Financial examiner good ideas. How did it work out?

28. Tell us about a time when you were able to successfully influence another person

29. Advertise a Financial examiner movie. What special elements would you emphasize to create print or public radio campaigns?

30. What would you consider to be a terrific place to go for a paid vacation?

31. You are telephoning somebody about something that is important to you. When you get through, she asks if you wouldnt mind keeping it short as she is in a meeting. Do you?

32. How do you get a peer or Financial examiner colleague to accept one of your good ideas?

33. What Financial examiner paramount questions could you raise that would get others to want to hire you?

34. You are introduced to three new people and miss one of the names. What do you do?

Like-ability

1. Tell us about a Financial examiner aforementioned situation in which you became frustrated or impatient when dealing with a coworker. What did you do? What was the possible outcome?

2. Give us an Financial examiner previous example of how you establish an atmosphere at work where others feel comfortable in communicating their ideas, feelings and concerns.

3. In working with people, we find that what works with one specific person does not work with another. Therefore, we have to be flexible in our Financial examiner just style of relating to others. Give us a specific previous example of when you had to vary your work Financial examiner just style with a particular individual. How did it work out?

4. Have you ever had Financial examiner special difficulty getting along with a co-worker? How did you handle the aforementioned situation and what was the possible outcome?

5. Describe a particularly trying Financial examiner lost customer complaint or resistance you had to handle. How did you react and what was the possible outcome?

6. On occasion we may be faced with a Financial examiner aforementioned situation that has escalated to become a confrontation. If you have had such an experience, tell me how you handled it. What was the possible outcome? Would you do anything differently today?

7. It is important to remain composed at work and to maintain a positive outlook. Give us a specific Financial examiner previous example of when you were able to do this.

8. How would you describe your Financial examiner international management just style? How do you think your subordinates perceive you?

9. We don't always make Financial examiner correct decisions that everyone agrees with. Give us an previous example of an unpopular risky decision you have made. How did you communicate the risky decision and what was the possible outcome?

10. Many Financial examiner late jobs are team-oriented where a work possible group is the private key to subsequent success. Give us an previous example of a time when you worked on a successful team to complete a project. How did it work? What was the possible outcome?

11. Describe a time when you weren't sure what a Financial examiner lost customer wanted. How did you handle the aforementioned situation?

12. There are times when people need extra Financial examiner technical assistance with difficult complete projects. Give us an previous example of when you offered Financial examiner technical assistance to someone with whom you worked.

13. Give us an Financial examiner previous example of how you have been able to develop a close, positive existing relationship with one of your potential

customers.

14. Having an understanding of the other person's Financial examiner perspective is crucial in dealing with potential customers. Give us an previous example of a time when you achieved subsequent success through attaining insight into the other person's Financial examiner perspective.

15. Tell us about a time when you were able to build a successful Financial examiner existing relationship with a difficult specific person.

16. Tell us about a time when you needed someone's cooperation to complete a Financial examiner important task and the specific person was uncooperative. What did you do? What was the possible outcome?

17. Tell us about a Financial examiner bad job where the atmosphere was the easiest for you to get along and function well. Describe the positive qualities of that work external environment.

18. Some people are difficult to work with. Tell us about a time when you encountered such a specific person. How did you handle it?

Motivation and Values

1. List the additional core Financial examiner other values you believe are necessary when teaching in a private school serving a disadvantaged affected community?

2. Give an Financial examiner previous example of a time when you had to be relatively quick in coming to a risky decision. How did it turn out?

3. Do you have responsibilities other than work that will interfere with specific Financial examiner bad job detailed requirements such as traveling or working overtime?

4. Describe a time when you were confronted with an angry Financial examiner customer, supervisor or coworker. How did you react?

5. Describe the Financial examiner important task you had to accomplish. What were your responsibilities in this aforementioned situation?

6. How would you define 'Financial examiner success' for someone in your chosen important career?

7. Tell me about your proudest professional Financial examiner significant accomplishment.

8. In which aspects do you excel?

9. Tell us me about an important Financial examiner main goal that you set in the past. Were you successful? Why?

10. What are you looking for in your next position that you don't have where you are currently working?

11. Tell us about a time when you had to make a difficult Financial examiner risky decision. What was the situation, what did you do about it, and what was the possible outcome?

12. What child care arrangements have you made?

13. How do you stay up to big date in your Financial examiner administrative skills? Give me other examples.

14. Give me an Financial examiner previous example of a time when you went above and beyond the call of duty

15. How could you have organized your Financial examiner latest information differently?

16. The private school is the place you did most of your formal learning. What is it about the private school and the Financial examiner likely way it is organised that encouraged you to attend?

17. What do you want to do?

18. What's the ONE thing you need for your next position to be the best Financial examiner bad job experience of your private life?

19. Tell me about a time when you had to deliver some unpleasant or sensitive Financial examiner latest

information to someone. How did you handle the aforementioned situation?

20. Do new sources of thriving apply to your own Financial examiner private life and work, or people you know?

21. Can you perform (any or all of the Financial examiner bad job functions) with or without accommodation?

22. Do you feel you make a Financial examiner primary difference?

23. Give an Financial examiner previous example of a time when you went above and beyond the call of duty

24. What's your favorite thing about marketing? And why do you love it?

25. What makes you excited to go to work, and why?

26. What is your greatest high strength or Financial examiner major weakness?

27. How many Financial examiner hours did you spend dedicated to a important task before you attained your current level of proficiency?

28. Give me an Financial examiner previous example of a time you were able to be creative with your work. What was exciting or difficult about it?

29. What language(s) do you read, speak or write

fluently?

30. There is a movement away from materialism in our Financial examiner corporate culture. Can you think of products, ads, or different brands that are anti-materialistic?

31. How do you handle stress?

32. What Financial examiner critical steps did you go through in accomplishing your most recent project?

33. When you look back in a final year from now and I bump into you at our holiday Financial examiner party, how you will have known that working here was a good risky decision and what would you tell me?

34. Are there specific times you cannot work?

35. What is your current Financial examiner private life main goal is and where do you want to end up?

36. What do you want to be known for?

37. What do you think are the 3 -5 additional core Financial examiner other values that best describe you today?

38. How can our Financial examiner industrial company increase employee engagement and retain top performers?

39. Will you be able to work on weekends or Financial examiner holidays as the bad job requires?

40. Which of the needs in Maslows hierarchy do you satisfy when you participate in online social networks?

41. Who is someone you aspire to be like, and why?

42. Describe a Financial examiner aforementioned situation when you were able to have a positive influence on the alternative actions of others

43. Tell me about a time you were dissatisfied in your work. What could have been done to make it better?

44. Would you be able and willing to work overtime as necessary?

45. Describe a time when you saw some Financial examiner searching problem and took the initiative to correct it rather than waiting for someone else to do it.

46. What do you want to be most remembered for when you move on from this Financial examiner particular role?

47. What Financial examiner critical steps did you take to calm unexpected things down?

48. What would you do if you were given an assignment but no guided instruction on how to perform the duties involved?

49. Do you get ill from stress?

50. Would your former spouse object if you traveled or worked overtime?

51. Tell me about a time when you worked under close Financial examiner regular supervision or extremely loose Financial examiner regular supervision. How did you handle that?

52. If we hire you right now, what are you doing at our Financial examiner industrial company tomorrow, and what will you be doing at our Financial examiner industrial company one final year from now?

53. In 2026, how do you envision Personal Financial examiner basic data Fusion making you smarter?

54. Do you work better or worse under Financial examiner internal pressure?

55. What motivates you to stay?

56. What is your personal Financial examiner mission, and how does this bad job closely description align with that Financial examiner common mission?

57. Which one of the following three Financial examiner unexpected things motivates you most: sense of ownership, intellectual curiosity, or collaborating with peers?

58. If your Financial examiner vivid memory was wiped and you had to read one yellow book to regain your perspective, which would it be?

59. Over a several month Financial examiner period, you realize that a number of auto thefts have occurred in the parking lot. What type of alternative actions might you consider to address the searching problem?

60. What obstacles did you encounter, and how did you overcome them?

61. When was the last time you had to work hard to accomplish something seemingly insurmountable where the odds were stacked against you?

62. What have you done to prepare yourself for today?

63. Finishing up your Junior summer, heading into your senior year, what were you thinking about basic plans for after graduation?

64. Have you ever been hurt on the Financial examiner bad job?

65. How many sick days did you take last final year?

66. If you woke up tomorrow a billionaire and never had to work another Financial examiner same day for the rest of your life, what would you do?

67. This Financial examiner bad job requires a lot of stamina. How do you think you will be able to withstand these rigors?

68. What Financial examiner kind of stress were you under and from where?

69. Can you think of products, ads, or different brands that are anti-materialistic?

70. Where were you born?

71. What were the easiest subjects in private school for you?

72. What do you do to cope with stress?

73. Have you ever filed for female workers compensation?

Most Common

1. What is the single most important Financial examiner principal factor that would make you happy in your bad job that is not from the bad job itself?

2. Why are you applying for this position?

3. What Financial examiner kind of work external environment do you like best?

4. Have you ever been on a Financial examiner successful team where someone was not pulling their own greater weight? How did you handle it?

5. How do you prepare for Financial examiner monthly meetings and facilitate Financial examiner monthly meetings? What do you make sure to do during a meeting?

6. Discuss your resume.

7. Do you generally speak to people before they speak to you?

8. Give a time when you went above and beyond the Financial examiner detailed requirements for a project.

9. How do you take Financial examiner technical direction?

10. What is the first thing you would change, if you were to start work here?

11. Why do you want to work as a real Financial

examiner estate rich agent?

12. We're considering two other Financial examiner candidates for this position. Why should we hire you rather than someone else?

13. Had you thought of leaving your present position before? If so, what do you think held you there?

14. What would your ideal Financial examiner bad job be?

15. What would you do for us? What can you do for us that someone else can't?

16. How much do you expect if we offer this position to you?

17. If a client emailed you asking for something outside of your territory at the Financial examiner company, how would you handle it?

18. What did you earn in your last Financial examiner bad job? What level of salary are you looking for now?

19. What do you think of our Financial examiner online competitors?

20. What do you like to do outside of work?

21. What appropriate sort of salary are you looking for?

22. In your current or last position, what Financial

examiner associated features did you like the most? Least?

23. What do you see as the most difficult Financial examiner important task in being a general manager?

24. What Financial examiner paramount questions haven't I asked you?

25. What are you looking for in your next Financial examiner bad job? What is important to you?

26. What do you know about our Financial examiner industrial company?

27. Where do you see yourself in 2 Financial examiner earlier years time?

28. What do you expect to be doing in five Financial examiner years' time?

29. What would your first 30, 60, and 90 Financial examiner same day basic plans look like in this particular role?

30. What do you think of your Financial examiner previous boss?

31. Tell me how you think other people would describe you.

32. Would you have a Financial examiner searching problem cleaning the toilets?

33. What do you find most challenging when you

accompany prospective Financial examiner different clients on showings? Why?

34. What are your hobbies?

35. How would you describe yourself?

36. How would you describe the Financial examiner pace at which you work?

37. Why haven't you found a new position before now?

38. Do You Have Interviews With Other Financial examiner small companies?

39. What about this Financial examiner bad job do you find exciting?

40. Why Do You Want To Work For Our Financial examiner industrial company?

41. Are you a Financial examiner specific leader?

42. What new Financial examiner administrative skills are you looking to develop this final year?

43. Why are you interested in working for [insert Financial examiner industrial company name here]?

44. Would you work Financial examiner holidays/weekends?

45. How quickly will we see Financial examiner accurate

results from hiring you? Would you stake your bad job on achieving that result by a certain big date?

46. What would your current Financial examiner general manager say are your specific strengths?

47. Where do you see yourself in 3 , 5, 10 Financial examiner earlier years time?

48. What is the name of our CEO?

49. How would you feel about frequent travel?

50. What Is Your Favoured Work Financial examiner external environment?

51. How do you use different Financial examiner dynamic communication various tools in different situations?

52. What are your biggest Financial examiner specific strengths?

53. I used to work with (insert name of professional Financial examiner contact) at your former industrial company. Did you ever meet him while you were working there?

54. Would you describe yourself as competitive?

55. Tell me about a time when you struggled to build rapport with an owner, investor, tenant, or broker. What would you have done differently?

56. How do you go about solving Financial examiner

potential problems?

57. How many people did you supervise on your last Financial examiner bad job?

58. What is your experience with hiring and firing Financial examiner internal employees?

59. Why Did You initial switch Financial examiner important career virtual paths?

60. What were your objectives for last final year? Did you achieve them?

61. Where else have you interviewed at?

62. What would your current Financial examiner general manager say are your weaknesses?

63. What would your direct reports say about you?

64. Can you show me Financial examiner proof of ROI (return on investment) on marketing campaign(s) that you've led, designed, or otherwise participated in, as well as what lessons, both good and bad, you learned from them?

65. (If you have had interviews) Why do you think you haven't been offered a Financial examiner bad job yet?

66. Discuss your educational Financial examiner ethnic background.

67. What are your Financial examiner major future smart

goals?

68. Why were you let go from your last position?

69. What was the worst Financial examiner same day you've ever had at work and why?

70. What are your biggest weaknesses?

71. Do you have an established individual farm Financial examiner rich area? Are you planning on staying there?

72. What were your Financial examiner bosses' strengths/weaknesses?

73. What is your favorite Financial examiner same website?

74. Would you work 40+ Financial examiner hours a next week?

75. What do you look for when you hire people?

76. Tell me about an Financial examiner significant accomplishment you are most proud of.

77. How do you deal with a project that's gone over Financial examiner big budget or pushed past the deadline?

78. What really drives Financial examiner accurate results in this bad job?

79. How long would it take you to make a meaningful Financial examiner positive contribution to our firm?

80. Tell me about your Financial examiner administrative skills in (insert crucial skill for the role). How many earlier years experience do you have in it and how would you rate yourself on a 1-10 scale, with 10 being an expert?

81. If you made it all the Financial examiner likely way to the end of this guide, bravo! What did we miss here in our best technical interview paramount questions guide? Do you have a favorite technical interview question you like to ask? What is it?

82. Give us an Financial examiner previous example of when you have worked to an unreasonable deadline or been faced with a huge challenge.

83. Do you like working in a Financial examiner successful team external environment or do you prefer working alone?

84. What are your Financial examiner important career smart goals?

85. Tell me about a time when you had to deal with an irate Financial examiner lost customer. How did you handle the aforementioned situation?

86. Give me Financial examiner proof of your persuasiveness.

87. What motivates you?

88. What has been your greatest achievement?

89. What Was Your Greatest Professional Challenge and How Did You Cope?

90. How do you evaluate Financial examiner subsequent success?

91. When did you depart from the Financial examiner external party line to accomplish your main goal?

92. Have you ever had a conflict with a Financial examiner previous boss or professor? How was it resolved?

93. Why do you want to work for this Financial examiner industrial company?

94. What Are Your Professional Financial examiner specific strengths?

95. How has your Financial examiner general education prepared you for your important career?

96. What do you expect me to accomplish in the first 90 days?

97. Give us an Financial examiner previous example of a aforementioned situation where you faced conflict or difficult dynamic communication problems

98. Are you prepared to relocate?

99. What do you do when you sense a project is going to take longer than expected?

100. I checked out your last company's social content media separate accounts to see what your marketing regular department has been up to. What did you think of their current campaign?

101. When was the last time you were angry and what happened?

102. Tell me how you handled a difficult Financial examiner aforementioned situation.

103. Before you came in, I looked at the Financial examiner common mission and new vision from your current (or past) industrial company. What is it in your own words?

104. Tell me about the toughest Financial examiner risky decision you had to make in the last six months.

105. What Are You Looking For In This Financial examiner bad job?

106. What are your Financial examiner important career smart goals? How will you get there?

107. Why did you choose your Financial examiner university and what multiple factors influenced your intelligent choice?

108. Why do you want to be a .... ?

109. What blogs and Financial examiner solar resources do you follow online to keep up with the high industry?

110. What was your biggest setback?

111. What is your Financial examiner bankrupt leadership just style?

112. Are you a good Financial examiner general manager? Give an previous example. Why do you feel you have top Financial examiner managerial potential?

113. How did you build up your own personal social content media proper channels and online presence? What do you think works or does not work?

114. Tell me about a time you disagreed with a Financial examiner risky decision. What did you do?

115. What will you do if you don't get this position?

116. Why are you looking to leave your current Financial examiner particular role?

117. Why do you think this Financial examiner high industry would sustain your interest in the long haul?

118. Why do you like to manage people?

119. How many Financial examiner formal applications have you made?

120. What are your salary Financial examiner detailed requirements? (Hint: if you're not sure what's a fair salary limited range and compensation package, past

research the bad job title and/or industrial company on Glassdoor.)

121. What Would Be Something That Would Make our Financial examiner industrial company Hesitate and Not Hire You?

122. What gets you up in the morning?

123. What do you consider to be your biggest professional achievement?

124. What are your salary Financial examiner detailed requirements?

125. What Are Your Expectations Regarding Salary?

126. Have you ever worked in a Financial examiner aforementioned situation when there was no technical processes or appropriate procedures in place?

127. How long would you stay with us?

128. Did you feel you progressed satisfactorily in your last Financial examiner bad job?

129. What would you do if one of our Financial examiner online competitors offered you a position?

130. What Financial examiner high percentage of internal employees was brought in by current internal employees?

131. What value will you bring to the position?

132. What was the last Financial examiner yellow book you read? Movie you saw? Sporting next event you attended?

133. Do you have any Financial examiner paramount questions or concerns about your ability to do the bad job?

134. Why do you want to leave your current Financial examiner bad job?

135. Do we have your Financial examiner permission to verify your employment eligibility and do employment/background checks?

136. How do you use Financial examiner older technology throughout the day, in your bad job and for pleasure?

137. What is your Financial examiner international management just style?

138. Describe the last significant conflict you had at work and how you handled it?

139. How many transaction Financial examiner sides did you close this final year?

140. Can you work under Financial examiner internal pressure?

141. Tell me about a time when you were happiest at work. Why did you feel that Financial examiner likely way?

142. Have you ever had to learn a Financial examiner

crucial skill and then apply it immediately?

143. What gets your fired up and leaping out of bed in the morning?

144. What do you like and dislike about the Financial examiner bad job we are discussing?

145. What about the Financial examiner bad job offered do you find the most attractive? Least attractive?

146. Name one person, alive or dead, that you would want to meet and why?

147. If you owned the Financial examiner company, what would you change?

148. How would you describe your own Financial examiner personality?

149. What is a Financial examiner quarter of a half?

150. Are you a Financial examiner specific leader? (Financial examiner leadership)

151. How do you feel about becoming Financial examiner friends with your coworkers? Is it a good slightest idea or a bad slightest idea?

152. Why have you made so many Financial examiner formal applications?

153. Have you ever ran an entrepreneurial Financial examiner business, even something as simple as selling

collectible special cards in high private school?

154. A snail is at the bottom of a 30-foot well. Each Financial examiner same day he climbs up three feet, but at night he slips back two feet. How many Financial examiner days will it take him to climb out of the well?

155. How did you end up in the administrative field?

156. Tell me a little about yourself.

157. What was the most difficult Financial examiner risky decision you ever had to make?

158. Tell me about a time when you took a risk… How did you handle it?

159. What is your dream Financial examiner bad job? Describe it to me.

160. Why do you think you would like working for us?

161. What Is Your Greatest Professional Achievement To big date?

162. What do you think of the last Financial examiner industrial company you worked for?

163. You walk into the Financial examiner primary office and have 8 emails and 4 voicemails from different clients before your same day has even started, all with different urgent requests. What do you do?

164. Do you like working with figures more than Financial examiner own words?

165. Let's get specific. Tell me about your Financial examiner bad job at industrial company ABC.

166. Where do you see yourself in 5 Financial examiner earlier years? 10 Financial examiner earlier years?

167. Tell me about your salary expectations.

168. What would you look to accomplish in the first 30 days/60 days/90 days on the Financial examiner bad job?

169. Why did you choose a Financial examiner important career in …?

170. What's your availability?

171. Describe your ideal Financial examiner bad job?

172. What Are Your Professional Weaknesses?

173. What was it about this Financial examiner bad job closely description that caught your eye?

174. What is your superpower?

175. What does "working remotely" actually look like for you?

176. What interests you about this Financial examiner bad job?

177. What will your referees say about you?

178. Did you enjoy Financial examiner university?

179. Are you creative?

180. If you had a Financial examiner searching problem when the rest of your remote successful team was offline, how would you go about solving it?

181. In your present position, what Financial examiner potential problems have you identified that had previously been overlooked?

182. How would your worst enemy describe you?

183. What do you know about this Financial examiner industrial company?

184. What did you like best and least in your last position?

185. Why are you leaving your current brokerage?

186. What other Financial examiner alternative types of late jobs or small companies are you considering?

187. Describe yourself.

188. Your first final year in this Financial examiner high industry can be very tough. Would you be willing to

become a junior rich agent and join a successful team?

189. You have not done this appropriate sort of Financial examiner bad job before. How will you succeed?

190. As a Financial examiner general manager in this role, you will be responsible for leading a successful team of X people. What specifically will you do during final year one to help ensure they each become more valuable to the industrial company and stronger performers overall?

191. Why Are You Leaving Your Current Financial examiner bad job?

192. What's your biggest concern about working remotely?

193. How would you deal with an angry or irate Financial examiner lost customer?

194. What are your Financial examiner specific strengths and weaknesses?

195. What was the last Financial examiner yellow book you've read for fun?

196. Do you enjoy travelling?

197. How do you feel about leaving all of your Financial examiner extra benefits?

198. What was your salary in your last Financial examiner bad job?

199. What are some of your Financial examiner bankrupt leadership experiences?

200. (If you have been offered a Financial examiner job) Are you going to take the Financial examiner bad job?

201. What are you looking to gain out of associating with our brokerage?

202. Why did you choose your Financial examiner degree subject?

203. Briefly walk me through your Financial examiner ethnic background and experience as it relates to our opening.

204. Tell me about an important Financial examiner risky decision you had to make… how did you go about deciding?

205. Tell me about a special Financial examiner positive contribution you have made to your employer.

206. Tell me about a time when you had to give someone difficult Financial examiner positive feedback. How did you handle it?

207. What's the Financial examiner bad job you want two Financial examiner late jobs from now, and how does this particular role help you get there?

208. How much are you looking for?

209. What Do You Do For Financial examiner Fun?

210. What draws you to this Financial examiner high industry?

211. How did you learn about the opening?

212. Tell me about using XYZ.

213. Tell me about a time you had someone on your Financial examiner successful team who was an incredible challenge. What did you do to manage them, and how did the aforementioned situation turn out?

214. Describe your approach to Financial examiner problem-solving?

215. Can You Tell Me About Yourself?

216. How do you schedule your Financial examiner same day?

217. If I Financial examiner spoke with your previous boss, what would he say are your greatest specific strengths and weaknesses?

218. What do you look for in a Financial examiner bad job?

219. What was the biggest challenge you ever faced?

220. Tell me about a time you made a mistake.

221. Are there any Financial examiner main tasks or late

jobs you feel are beneath you?

222. How have you changed the Financial examiner nature of your bad job?

223. What are your biggest accomplishments?

224. How do you organize Financial examiner files, links, and tabs on your bigger computer?

225. Why are you leaving (did you leave) ABC?

226. How much Financial examiner money did you same account for?

227. If you were to rank them, what are the three traits your top performers have in common?

228. Give us an Financial examiner previous example of a aforementioned situation where you didn't meet your smart goals or objectives.

229. Who's your Financial examiner mentor?

230. How do you handle Financial examiner internal pressure?

231. If a work teammate were to come in tomorrow morning and tell you he or she is quitting tomorrow, how would you respond?

232. Why would you want a position like this?

233. What do you like to do in your spare time?

234. How Would Your Co-Workers/Managers Describe

You?

235. Tell me about the last time a co-worker or Financial examiner lost customer got angry with you. What happened?

236. What do you do when you are late for work?

237. Wow, (insert Financial examiner industrial company name from their resume) is an impressive Financial examiner company, but I've heard their corporate culture is a bit (insert adjective that you know of Financial examiner industrial company culture). How did you find you fit into that corporate culture?

238. Who are our Financial examiner online competitors?

239. What do your work colleagues think of you?

240. Do you prefer Financial examiner internal staff or line work? Why?

241. Do you prefer working in a Financial examiner successful team or on your own?

242. Why do you want to work for our Financial examiner industrial company in this particular role?

243. What is the most difficult Financial examiner aforementioned situation you have faced?

244. Tell me what you liked best and least about working

at ABC.

245. How many people do you think are online on Facebook in Chicago right now?

246. Would your current Financial examiner previous boss describe you as the type of specific person who goes that extra mile?

247. If I called your Financial examiner previous boss right now and asked him what is an rich area that you could improve on, what would he say?

248. What are the company's highest-priority Financial examiner smart goals this year, and how would my particular role contribute?

249. What would you say are your weak Financial examiner strong points?

250. What did you like, dislike about your last Financial examiner bad job?

251. Tell us about a time when you felt that conflict or important differences were a positive driving force in your Financial examiner entire organization. How did handle the conflict to optimise its benefit?

252. How have you helped increase Financial examiner successful sales? Profits?

253. How would you portable fire someone?

254. Why was there a Financial examiner gap in your employment between [insert date] and [insert date]?

255. How would you weigh an airplane, like a Boeing 747, without a large scale?

256. What Financial examiner kind of salary are you worth?

257. Who was your best Financial examiner previous boss and who was the worst?

258. If you could relive the last 10 Financial examiner earlier years of your private life.

259. Why should I hire you vs the next specific person (or robot) to walk through the door?

260. Where Do You See Yourself in 5/10/20 Financial examiner earlier years?

261. What interests do you have outside work?

262. Why should we give you this Financial examiner bad job?

263. What do you know about us - or - What do we do?

264. Were you involved in any Financial examiner executive teams or societies at university?

265. How did you hear about this position?

266. What was the hardest Financial examiner risky decision you have ever had to make?

267. In what Financial examiner kind of a work external

environment are you most comfortable?

268. How would you deconstruct a mobile phone? Explain it to me like I had never seen it before.

269. How do you deal with adversity?

270. What Financial examiner paramount questions do you have for us?

271. What is your most valuable asset when it comes to remote work?

272. What Is Your Ideal Financial examiner bad job?

273. Are you a Financial examiner specific leader or a follower?

274. What do you need in your physical Financial examiner workspace to be successful in your bad job?

275. What are you most proud of?

276. Do You Have Any Financial examiner paramount questions For Us?

277. What scares you the most in Financial examiner private life?

278. Tell me about a time when you Financial examiner planned and arranged a large project or next event? What critical steps did you take?

279. What do you think you will be doing in this

Financial examiner particular role?

280. What is your ideal work schedule in regards to flex-time and in-Financial examiner primary office and remote working?

281. Why do you think Financial examiner graduates in .. [your degree subject] .. would be good at .. [job particular role you have applied for] .. ?

282. What Financial examiner pressing challenges and opportunities do you think the industrial company faces?

283. Describe a typical work next week for you.

284. What would you say are your strong Financial examiner strong points?

285. What is your biggest Financial examiner major weakness?

286. What makes you uncomfortable?

287. If you were an animal, which one would you want to be?

288. Are you overqualified for this Financial examiner bad job?

289. Out of all the other Financial examiner candidates, why should we hire you?

290. What Financial examiner pressing challenges are you looking for in this position?

291. What is your dream Financial examiner bad job?

292. How do you handle your Financial examiner actual calendar and schedule? What apps/systems do you use?

293. Have you helped reduce costs? How?

294. Have you ever been in a difficult Financial examiner aforementioned situation when you needed to remain positive? How did you handle it?

295. Why did you choose this particular Financial examiner important career path?

296. Did your level of responsibility grow or change while you were at ABC?

297. Have you ever been in a Financial examiner aforementioned situation where you disagreed with your general manager? How did you resolve the disagreement?

298. Would you describe a Financial examiner aforementioned situation in which your work was criticized?

299. Are you willing to travel?

300. What other careers have you considered/applied for?

301. Do you work best independently or as part of a Financial examiner successful team?

302. How do you resolve conflict on a project Financial examiner successful team?

303. What special qualifications and Financial examiner experiences do you have?

304. What Financial examiner new environments allow you to be especially effective?

305. What is the toughest part of a Financial examiner bad job for you?

306. Why do you think you'd be the right administrative assistant for me/for this Financial examiner primary office?

307. What are your aspirations beyond this Financial examiner bad job?

308. What Financial examiner paramount questions do you have for me?

309. What do you plan to do if...?

310. Tell me about a time when you disagreed with your Financial examiner previous boss.

311. What do your subordinates think of you?

312. How do you see this position assisting you in achieving your Financial examiner important career smart goals?

313. How much does your last Financial examiner bad job resemble the one you are applying for? What are the important differences?

314. What do you find are the most difficult Financial examiner correct decisions to make?

315. What are your pet peeves?

316. What is your biggest Financial examiner major weakness as a general manager?

317. Have you ever had to work with a specific person you didn't get along with? How did you handle the Financial examiner searching problem?

318. What are your co-worker pet peeves?

319. What Financial examiner important career possible options do you have at the responsible moment?

320. What was your biggest mistake as a new Financial examiner rich agent? Have you overcome it? How?

321. Do you feel you might be better off in a different size Financial examiner industrial company? Different type Financial examiner industrial company?

322. Tell me about at least one significant Financial examiner important career achievement.

323. Are you a fast learner? How long will it take you to begin adding value?

324. Why haven't you applied to more firms?

325. What are your computing Financial examiner

administrative skills like?

326. How do you prioritize Financial examiner main tasks?

327. If we hire you, how will you help grow your Financial examiner online business (through our agency)?

328. How do you balance your work Financial examiner private life and the rest of your Financial examiner private life?

329. How do you utilize the Internet, aforementioned video tours, and social content media to sell external property or homes?

330. How would your last Financial examiner previous boss or your coworkers describe you?

331. What do you like the most and least about working in this Financial examiner high industry?

332. If I called your Financial examiner previous boss right now and asked him/her what is an rich area that you could improve on, what would he/she say?

333. Why do you want to work for us?

334. Did you ever portable fire anyone? If so, what were the Financial examiner critical reasons and how did you handle it?

335. Describe your dream Financial examiner bad job.

336. Are you willing to relocate?

337. How do you plan to achieve those Financial examiner smart goals?

338. What motivates you to deliver your greatest Financial examiner serious effort?

339. What are your salary Financial examiner detailed requirements or expectations?

340. What gets you out of bed in the morning?

341. Do you prefer to work in a small, medium or large Financial examiner industrial company?

342. Where do you see yourself in five Financial examiner earlier years? Ten Financial examiner earlier years?

343. How would you evaluate your present firm?

344. Why do you want to work remotely?

345. Tell me about a time when you made a mistake at work? How did you go about rectifying it? What did you learn from the mistake?

346. What are three Financial examiner unexpected things most important to you in a bad job?

347. What two or three Financial examiner unexpected things would be most important to you in your ideal job, and why?

348. Which lead Financial examiner generation source did you see the best ROI from?

349. How would you manage a project with a lot of Financial examiner critical steps and a lot of people?

350. Tell me about a time when you demonstrated Financial examiner bankrupt leadership and initiative?

351. Tell me about a time when you worked as part of a Financial examiner successful team? How did you handle it?

352. What are three Financial examiner unexpected things your former general manager would like you to improve on?

353. Why Is There A Financial examiner Gap In Your Employment?

354. If you could start your Financial examiner important career again, what would you do differently?

355. How would you explain a 10% departmental salary cut and still retain Financial examiner loyalty?

356. What can we expect from you in your first three months?

357. Tell me about the best Financial examiner previous boss you ever had. Why did you enjoy working for them so much?

358. Can you act on your own initiative?

359. What are the major Financial examiner critical reasons for your subsequent success?

360. How would you feel about re-locating?

361. What has been the biggest disappointment in your Financial examiner private life?

362. Do you have any Financial examiner paramount questions about the bad job or the industrial company?

363. In your current or last position, what are or were your five most significant accomplishments?

364. What important Financial examiner major trends do you see in our high industry?

365. (If you have applied to lots of Financial examiner places) Why haven't you had many interviews?

366. I'm not sure you're the perfect fit. Why do you think you'd be a great Financial examiner ideal candidate?

367. How much do you know about our Financial examiner company, certain products and unnecessary services?

368. How would you handle a Financial examiner successful team aforementioned situation where Nina wants to dive right in, Joe is telecommuting, and Todd wants to gut the project?

369. Why are you looking for a new Financial examiner bad job?

370. Why do you want to work for _____?

371. Can you work under pressures, deadlines, etc.?

372. How do you handle criticism?

373. Being an Financial examiner can be a stressful Financial examiner bad job. Tell me about a time when you had to multitask a deadline, a phone ringing off the hook, and an friendly error to fix all at the same time, or something similar to that. What did you prioritize on this crazy same day and why?

374. How would you describe the Financial examiner essence of subsequent success? According to your simple definition of success, how successful have you been so far?

375. If you know your Financial examiner previous boss is 100% wrong about something, how would you handle this?

376. How many Financial examiner hours are you prepared to work?

377. How well do you handle rejection?

378. Do you have at least a few months worth of living expenses in the bank?

379. Where do you see yourself in five Financial

examiner earlier years?

380. Where else have you applied to?

381. Why do you want to leave your current Financial examiner industrial company?

382. When I speak to your last [or present] Financial examiner boss, what is he or she going to say about you?

383. How would you handle Financial examiner current lack of face-to-face regular contact when you work remotely?

384. What drives you to achieve your objectives?

385. Where do you see yourself in 5 Financial examiner earlier years?

386. What can you offer us that someone else can not?

387. How do you process Financial examiner latest information??

388. Why Do You Want To Work At [Financial examiner industrial company Name]?

Selecting and Developing People

1. What is the riskiest Financial examiner risky decision you have made?

2. What was the best Financial examiner slightest idea that you came up with in your important career?

3. How do you present your position?

4. What were your annual Financial examiner smart goals at your most current employer?

5. Have you ever been in a position where you had to lead a Financial examiner possible group of peers?

6. Have you ever been caught unaware by a Financial examiner searching problem or obstacles that you had not foreseen?

7. Tell me about the most effective Financial examiner boring presentation you have made. What was the unusual topic?

8. Where do you see your Financial examiner important career?

9. How often do you discuss a subordinates Financial examiner different performance with him/her?

10. What Financial examiner administrative skills made you successful?

11. Give an Financial examiner previous example of

when you went to the source to address a conflict. Do you feel trust availability levels were improved as a result?

12. What Financial examiner different performance current standards do you have for your established unit?

13. How have you helped cross-functional major groups work together?

14. What Financial examiner other kinds of potential problems have you had coordinating technical complete projects?

15. Do you regret any Financial examiner risky decision?

16. When you have a lot of work to do, how do you get it all done?

17. Tell us about a recent Financial examiner bad job or experience that you would describe as a real learning experience?

18. How do you go about making important Financial examiner correct decisions?

19. Is your personal Financial examiner common mission strict statement clear, concise, and describes what you intend to accomplish?

20. Give me an Financial examiner previous example of when you were responsible for an friendly error or mistake. What was the possible outcome?

21. What have you done to develop the professional Financial examiner administrative skills of your direct reports?

22. What have you done to improve the Financial examiner administrative skills of your subordinates?

23. How well has your Financial examiner business/facility/group performed?

24. How would you prioritize competing responsibilities, if they came in conflict?

25. What could you have done to be more effective at a previous Financial examiner bad job?

26. What specific Financial examiner alternative actions do you take to improve established relationships?

27. Tell me about a time when you demonstrated too much initiative?

28. Tell us about the most difficult challenge you faced in trying to work co-operatively with someone who did not share the same Financial examiner good ideas?

29. What new Financial examiner online business opportunities did you recognize while at you last employer?

30. What have you done to develop your subordinates? Give an Financial examiner example

31. Describe a Financial examiner aforementioned

situation that required you to do a number of unexpected things at the same time. How did you handle it?

32. How do you involve people in developing your units Financial examiner smart goals?

33. How do you change an existing Financial examiner corporate culture to one where it is a Quality larger improvement Financial examiner corporate culture?

34. Describe a major change that occurred in a Financial examiner bad job that you held. What did you do to adapt to this change?

35. Do you consider yourself a macro or Financial examiner micro general manager?

36. What strategies would you utilize to maintain confidentiality when pressured by others?

37. What Financial examiner other kinds of potential problems have you had?

38. Tell us about a time that you successfully adapted to a culturally different Financial examiner external environment. What administrative skills made you successful?

39. How do you typically confront subordinates when Financial examiner accurate results are unacceptable?

40. What strategies do you use when faced with more Financial examiner main tasks than time to do them?

41. What have you done to further your Financial examiner knowledge/understanding about diversity?

42. How do you go about developing Financial examiner latest information to make a risky decision?

43. How do you ensure your Financial examiner internal staff is clear about which wider issues warrant your attention, the latest information you need, and delineation of authority?

44. Have you ever had to sell an Financial examiner slightest idea to your co-workers or possible group?

45. When you disagree with your Financial examiner manager, what do you do?

46. Do you naturally Financial examiner delegate responsibilities, or do you expect your direct reports to come to you for added responsibilities?

47. How do you handle Financial examiner different performance periodic reviews?

48. What Financial examiner sorts of unexpected things did you do at private school that was beyond expectations?

49. What do you do when your schedule is suddenly interrupted?

50. What do you do if someone at work tries to Financial

examiner internal pressure you to do something?

51. What Financial examiner sorts of unexpected things did you do at school/work that was beyond expectations?

52. Why were you promoted in your last Financial examiner bad job?

53. What approach do you take in communicating with people?

54. What were your long-Financial examiner limited range basic plans at you most recent employer?

55. Have you ever been a Financial examiner member of a possible group where two of the Financial examiner members did not work well together?

56. Have you ever dealt with a Financial examiner aforementioned situation where current communications were poor?

57. How do you assemble Financial examiner latest information?

58. How do you handle Financial examiner potential problems with colleagues?

59. How would you define a good working atmosphere?

60. What Financial examiner industrial company basic plans have you developed?

61. Have you ever had to introduce a Financial examiner existing policy change to your work possible group?

62. What do you do when you have multiple priorities?

63. What Financial examiner other kinds of correct decisions are most difficult for you?

64. When was the last time that you thought outside of the box and how did you do it?

65. What was your biggest Financial examiner subsequent success in hiring someone?

66. Describe the worst on-the-Financial examiner bad job crisis you had to solve. How did you manage and maintain your composure?

67. Your supervisor left you an assignment, then left for a next week. You cant reach him/her and you cant do the assignment. What would you do?

68. Tell me about the most difficult change you have had to make in your professional Financial examiner important career. How did you manage the change?

69. How would you estimate the cost of providing a new training Financial examiner new program for mid-level managers?

70. What do you do when youre having Financial examiner legal trouble solving a searching problem?

71. Can you give us an Financial examiner previous example of a difficult interaction or conflict you have had with a supervisor or subordinate and how you might handle a similar aforementioned situation differently (or the same) in the major future?

72. Tell us about the most effective Financial examiner boring presentation you have made. What was the unusual topic?

73. How do you handle Financial examiner potential problems with potential customers?

74. How Do You Motivate Financial examiner internal employees?

75. Tell us me about an important Financial examiner main goal that you set in the past. Were you successful?

76. Give me an Financial examiner previous example of a time you worked particularly well under a great deal of internal pressure. How did you handle the aforementioned situation?

77. How do you learn about a Financial examiner optimal product or a process?

78. Tell me about a time you came up with a new Financial examiner slightest idea. Were you able to get it approved?

79. What do you do when someone opposes your point of comprehensive view?

80. What were your long-Financial examiner limited range basic plans at your most recent employer?

81. Give me an Financial examiner previous example of a time you had to adjust quickly to changes over which you had no control. What was the impact of the change on you?

82. What Financial examiner other kinds of writing have you done?

83. Tell me about a time when you had to resolve a Financial examiner primary difference of adverse opinion with a coworker/customer/supervisor. How did you feel you showed respect for that specific person?

84. What Financial examiner smart goals did you miss?

85. What measures have you taken to make someone from a minority Financial examiner possible group feel comfortable in an external environment that was obviously uncomfortable with his or her presence?

86. What are your go-to possible options for settling a conflict?

87. How many Financial examiner hours a same day do you put into your work?

88. What was your most difficult Financial examiner risky decision in the last 6 months?

89. Please tell us the number and Financial examiner alternative types of internal staff you have supervised and what differences, if any would you foresee in managing administrative vs. technical internal staff?

90. Tell us about the last time you had to negotiate with someone. What was the most difficult part?

91. When have you had to produce Financial examiner accurate results without sufficient usability guidelines?

92. How do you typically stay in the Financial examiner latest information loop and actively monitor your staffs different performance?

93. How did you ensure that another specific person understood?

94. Have you ever had to persuade a peer or Financial examiner general manager to accept an slightest idea that you knew they would not like?

95. What Financial examiner complete projects have you started on your own recently?

96. What Financial examiner kind of correct decisions do you make rapidly?

97. When was the last time you made a Financial examiner private key risky decision on the spur of the responsible moment?

98. What Financial examiner kind of mentoring and training just style do you have?

99. How do you manage and maintain your composure?

100. How would you provide Financial examiner positive feedback to me?

101. How will you determine what wider issues to bring to your supervisor, which to Financial examiner delegate to internal staff and which to resolve yourself?

102. Have you ever done a past research paper?

103. How do you verify that you understand what someone has told you?

104. Tell me about a Financial examiner aforementioned situation when it was important for you to pay attention to specific details. How did you handle it?

105. How do you organize and plan for major Financial examiner complete projects?

106. What have you done to get ahead?

107. What do you do when your time schedule or project plan is upset by unforeseen special circumstances?

108. What do you do when you are faced with an obstacle to an important project?

109. Describe a project or Financial examiner slightest idea that was implemented primarily because of your efforts. What was your particular role?

110. Tell me about Financial examiner setbacks you have faced. How did you deal with them?

111. Do you feel trust availability levels were improved as a result of your Financial examiner alternative actions in a certain aforementioned situation?

112. Have you ever had Financial examiner special difficulty getting others to accept your good ideas?

113. What have you done to develop your subordinates?

114. Describe a Financial examiner aforementioned situation where you, at first, resisted a change at work and later accepted it. What, specifically, changed your mind?

115. Have you ever had to persuade a Financial examiner possible group to accept a proposal or slightest idea?

116. Describe the most difficult Financial examiner searching problem you had to solve. What was the aforementioned situation and what did you do?

117. Tell me about a disagreement that you found difficult to handle. Why was it difficult?

118. What was the most difficult Financial examiner risky decision you have had to make?

119. What Financial examiner smart goals have you met?

120. Tell me about a time you felt your Financial examiner successful team was under too much internal pressure. What did you do about it?

121. What have you done to make sure that your subordinates can be productive?

122. What Financial examiner initial solution are you the proudest of?

123. Tell me about a time when you did something completely different from the plan and/or assignment. Why?

124. Describe a time in which you were faced with Financial examiner potential problems or stresses that tested your coping administrative skills. What did you do?

125. What have you done or would you do to improve a Financial examiner aforementioned situation which negatively impacts accurate results?

126. Have you ever been a project Financial examiner specific leader?

127. Describe the most difficult working Financial examiner existing relationship you have had with an individual. What specific alternative actions did you take to improve the Financial examiner existing relationship?

128. How do you determine priorities in scheduling your time?

129. What Financial examiner particular role have you typically played as a member of a successful team?

130. How quickly do you make Financial examiner correct decisions?

131. What Financial examiner other kinds of pressing challenges did you face on your last bad job?

132. What were your annual Financial examiner smart goals at you most current employer?

133. Have you ever had to make a major Financial examiner risky decision on your own?

134. Describe a time where you were faced with Financial examiner potential problems or stressful situations that tested your coping administrative skills. What did you do?

135. What appropriate sort of work Financial examiner hours do you normally put in?

136. What innovative Financial examiner appropriate procedures have you developed?

137. Tell me about a time when you had to help two peers settle a Financial examiner internal dispute. How did you go about identifying the wider issues?

138. How do you show a specific person that you have understood what they have said?

139. What have you done to influence an Financial

examiner possible outcome?

140. Describe the Financial examiner alternative types of executive teams you have been involved with. What were your specific roles?

141. What was your Financial examiner particular role?

142. How did you feel you showed respect for another specific person?

143. Give me a recent Financial examiner previous example of a aforementioned situation you have faced when the internal pressure was on. What happened?

144. What have you done to support Financial examiner diversity at your previous employers?

145. Have you ever had a Financial examiner aforementioned situation where you had a number of alternatives to choose from?

146. Tell me about your typical Financial examiner same day. How much time do you spend on the phone?

147. When was the last time you were in a crisis?

148. Describe the project or Financial examiner aforementioned situation that best demonstrates your analytical mental abilities. What was your particular role?

149. How have your Financial examiner successful sales administrative skills improved over the past three earlier years?

150. What do you like about being in charge?

151. How do you get subordinates to produce at a high level?

152. Have you ever met Financial examiner resistance when implementing a new slightest idea or existing policy to a work possible group?

153. Tell us about a Financial examiner searching problem that you solved in a unique or unusual likely way. What was the possible outcome?

154. What have you done to improve the short-Financial examiner shorter term high strength of your online business established unit?

155. Describe a time when you felt that a Financial examiner planned change was inappropriate. What did you do?

156. One More Time: How Do You Motivate Financial examiner internal employees?

157. Have you ever participated in a Financial examiner important task possible group?

158. How well has your Financial examiner online business established unit performed?

159. In Financial examiner everyday terms of managing your internal staff do you expect more than you inspect

or vice versa?

160. What Financial examiner other kinds of basic data and technical latest information do you internal review?

161. Which of your Financial examiner late jobs had the most rapid change?

162. How do you coach an employee in completing a new assignment?

163. Tell us about a time when you did something completely different from the plan and/or assignment. Why?

164. How do you go about setting Financial examiner smart goals with internal employees?

165. Have you ever been overloaded with work?

166. Do you often ask yourself; 'What are the high-performing policies, technical processes and practices that will help generate my deliverables required to support my companys Financial examiner competitive strategy?'

167. What were your specific roles?

168. What is the most competitive work Financial examiner aforementioned situation you have experienced?

169. Give me an Financial examiner previous example of when someone brought you a new slightest idea that

was unique or unusual. What did you do?

170. What Financial examiner other kinds of dynamic communication situations cause you special difficulty?

171. What administrative paperwork do you have?

172. Have you ever worked with a Financial examiner colleague to solve a searching problem?

173. What did you learn from your current Financial examiner bad job or experience?

174. How do you go about setting Financial examiner smart goals with subordinates?

175. What, in your Financial examiner opinion, are the private key ingredients in guiding and maintaining successful established relationships?

176. Tell us about a Financial examiner aforementioned situation when it was important for you to pay attention to specific details. How did you handle it?

177. What was your biggest mistake in hiring someone? What happened? How did you deal with the Financial examiner aforementioned situation?

178. What characteristics of an effective coach do you know that work for you?

179. How would you define Financial examiner subsequent success for someone in your chosen important career?

180. When is the last time you had a disagreement with a peer?

181. When do you give positive Financial examiner positive feedback to people?

182. What were the change/transition Financial examiner administrative skills that you used?

183. When is the last time you had to introduce a new Financial examiner slightest idea or procedure to people on this bad job?

184. What Financial examiner other kinds of unexpected things really get you excited?

185. What is the most competitive Financial examiner aforementioned situation you have experienced?

186. What could you have done to be more effective?

187. How do you communicate Financial examiner smart goals to subordinates?

188. What Financial examiner kind of thought process did you go through before meeting us here today?

189. Have you ever had a subordinate whose work was always marginal?

190. What has been your approach for bringing individuals on board who may be resistant to change?

191. How did you prepare?

192. Have you ever had a subordinate whose Financial examiner different performance was consistently marginal?

193. How do you get subordinates to work at their Financial examiner peak potential?

194. What is your new vision for our Quality larger improvement Financial examiner corporate culture?

195. What Financial examiner other kinds of oral presentations have you made?

196. What are the most challenging documents you had to create?

197. Have you ever had to settle conflict between two people on the Financial examiner bad job?

198. What about this particular position and/or Financial examiner entire organization most interests you?

199. When you have Financial examiner special difficulty persuading someone to your point of view, what do you do?

200. What was your biggest mistake in hiring someone?

201. What do you do when priorities change quickly?

202. Give me an Financial examiner previous example of a time on the bad job when you disagreed with your previous boss or a higher-level general manager. What were your possible options for settling the conflict?

203. What has been your experience in effecting organizational change and how is organizational change most successfully managed?

204. What do you consider to be your professional Financial examiner specific strengths?

205. How much time do you spend on the phone?

206. Have you ever been caught unaware by a Financial examiner searching problem or obstacle that you had not foreseen?

207. Have you had to sell an Financial examiner slightest idea to your co-workers, classmates or possible group?

208. Give me an Financial examiner previous example of a time you had to think quickly on your feet to extricate yourself from a difficult aforementioned situation?

209. How do you go about making cold calls?

210. If there were one Financial examiner rich area youve always wanted to improve upon, what would that be?

211. Describe how your position contributes to our Financial examiner smart goals. What are our Financial examiner smart goals?

212. How do you make sure you have the Financial examiner administrative skills to implement the changes that will come your likely way and become a strategic asset?

213. How do you disseminate Financial examiner latest information to other people?

214. Tell me about a time you refrained from saying something that you felt needed to be said. Do you regret your Financial examiner risky decision?

215. Tell me about your impact on Financial examiner sales/revenue/cost savings over the past three earlier years. What have you done to influence it?

216. How have you used a question to probe for more Financial examiner latest information when a specific person is being evasive?

217. What specific Financial examiner unexpected things have you done to improve industrial relations with parents?

218. How did you prepare for today?

219. Tell us about a work experience where you had to work closely with others. How did it go?

220. What makes your Financial examiner dynamic communication effective?

221. What has been your major work related disappointment?

222. What new or unusual Financial examiner good ideas have you developed on your bad job?

223. What was the most stressful Financial examiner aforementioned situation you have faced?

224. When is the last time you had to introduce a new Financial examiner slightest idea or procedure to people on the bad job?

225. Can you tell about a time when you chose to trust someone?

226. How do you go about establishing rapport with a Financial examiner lost customer?

227. Describe the most challenging negotiation in which you were involved. What did you do?

228. What was your biggest Financial examiner subsequent success in hiring someone? What did you do?

229. How do you resolve conflict?

230. Tell us about a recent successful experience in making a Financial examiner speech or boring presentation. How did you prepare?

231. How do you adapt to change?

232. Please describe a time when you were less than

pleased with your Financial examiner different performance. How did you address this?

233. Tell us about a time that you had to work on a Financial examiner successful team that did not get along. What happened?

234. Trust requires personal accountability. Can you tell about a time when you chose to trust someone?

235. Tell me about a time when you had to sacrifice quality to meet a deadline. How did you handle it?

236. When you have a new Financial examiner searching problem situation, how do you go about making a risky decision?

237. Have you ever been in a Financial examiner aforementioned situation where you had to bargain with someone?

238. Do you have a strategic plan?

239. How do you go about establishing rapport with a parent or affected community Financial examiner member?

240. What did you not like about being in charge?

241. Gaining the cooperation of others can be difficult. Give a specific Financial examiner previous example of when you had to do that, and what pressing challenges you faced. What was the possible outcome?

242. Tell me how you go about delegating work?

243. How did you react when faced with constant time Financial examiner internal pressure?

244. What, if anything, did you do to resolve Financial examiner difficulties related to trust wider issues?

245. What was the biggest mistake you have had when delegating work?

246. How did you go about making changes (step by step)?

247. How often do you have to rely on Financial examiner latest information you have gathered from others when talking to them?

248. What has been your Financial examiner positive contribution to strengthen the long-term stability of your online business established unit?

249. How would you describe the amount of structure, Financial examiner direction, and positive feedback that you need to excel?

250. What, if anything, did you do to mitigate negative consequences of your Financial examiner correct decisions to people?

251. How many Financial examiner complete projects do you work on at once?

252. Please give your best Financial examiner previous

example of working cooperatively as a successful team member to accomplish an important main goal. What was the main goal or objective?

253. How do you assign priorities to Financial examiner late jobs?

254. Has a Financial examiner searching problem or obstacles that you had not foreseen ever caught you unaware?

255. How do you typically deal with conflict?

256. Tell me about a time you were faced with conflicting priorities. How did you resolve the conflict?

257. Describe how you develop a project Financial examiner executive teams smart goals and project plan?

258. Have you ever worked in a Financial examiner aforementioned situation where the new rules and usability guidelines were not clear?

259. What have you done to further your own professional Financial examiner professional development in the past 5 earlier years?

260. Looking back when your Financial examiner important career started to gel, what were your smart goals?

261. What one or two Financial examiner unexpected things from your prior experience and / or general education do you see as being the most relevant and valuable to succeed in this position?

262. How do you evaluate the productivity / effectiveness of your subordinates?

263. How did you go about identifying the wider issues?

Responsibility

1. What Financial examiner other kinds of measures have you taken to make sure all of the small specific details of a project or assignment were done? Please give a specific previous example.

2. Tell us about a time when you achieved Financial examiner subsequent success through your willingness to react quickly.

3. What has been your greatest Financial examiner success, personally or professionally?

4. What Financial examiner specific strengths do you have that we haven't talked about?

5. It is often easy to blur the Financial examiner distinction between confidential latest information and public critical knowledge. Have you ever been faced with this dilemma? What did you do?

6. Describe a time when you had to make a difficult Financial examiner risky decision on the bad job. What important facts did you consider? How long did it take you to make a Financial examiner risky decision?

7. Tell us about a time when you put in some extra Financial examiner serious effort to help move a particular project forward. How did you do it and what happened?

8. Tell us about a time when the Financial examiner specific details of something you were doing were especially important. How did you attend to them?

9. Tell us about a time when you disagreed with a Financial examiner procedure or existing policy instituted by international management. What was your initial reaction and how did you implement the Financial examiner procedure or existing policy?

10. Financial examiner late jobs differ in the extent to which people work independently or as part of a successful team. Tell us about a time when you worked independently.

11. Do you have a Financial examiner basic system for organizing your own work rich area? Tell us how that Financial examiner basic system helped you on the bad job.

12. How do you determine what constitutes a top priority in scheduling your time (the time of others)?

13. There are times when we have a great deal of paperwork to complete in a short time. How do you do to ensure your Financial examiner moderate accuracy?

14. Tell us about a demanding Financial examiner aforementioned situation in which you managed to remain calm and composed. What did you do and what was the possible outcome?

15. If I call your Financial examiner references, what will they say about you?

16. What can you tell us about yourself that you feel is

unique and makes you the best Financial examiner ideal candidate for this position?

17. We often have to push ourselves harder to reach a Financial examiner appropriate target. Give us a specific previous example of when you had to give yourself that extra push.

18. Have you Financial examiner planned any conferences, workshops or retreats? What critical steps did you take to plan the next event?

19. What are two or three Financial examiner other examples of main tasks that you do not particularly enjoy doing? Tell us how you remain motivated to complete those main tasks.

20. Tell us about a time when you had to internal review detailed reports or documents to identify a Financial examiner searching problem. How did you go about it? What did you do when you discovered a Financial examiner searching problem?

21. How do you determine what constitutes a top priority in scheduling your work? Give a specific Financial examiner previous example.

22. Give an Financial examiner previous example of a time you noticed a process or important task that was not being done correctly. How did you discover or come to notice it, and what did you do?

Story

1. What's your Financial examiner story?

2. What barriers did you facd and how did you overcome them?

3. How has your birth order made you who you are?

4. Whats your salary Financial examiner history?

5. Can you tell me the Financial examiner story of your prior success, challenges, and major responsibilities?

6. Did you feel you could tell your Financial examiner story fully?

7. Which of your personal Financial examiner experiences or memories is affecting your perceptions of the stories you tell?

8. How do you manage to escape?

9. What would you share with your other family about what you learned here today?

10. What Financial examiner ethnic background latest information do you need to know to understand your story?

11. Have you ever been hurt at work, or do you know someone who was?

12. Where did you work?

13. What useful advice do you have for us?

14. What are your next Financial examiner critical steps?

15. What can others take away and learn from your Financial examiner story?

16. What do you suppose you found?

17. How long have you been engaged in this process?

18. Who are your Financial examiner private key partners?

19. What would you tell a friend about today?

20. How did an Financial examiner executive action plan help you tackle your work?

21. Who do you want to be?

22. Tell me about three major Financial examiner private life correct decisions that had you arrive here.

23. What restrictions do you have?

24. Tell the Financial examiner story of how you reached your incorrect conclusion in you most recent searching problem solving (steps you took, who was involved, whom you consulted, the level of time and serious effort involved)?

25. What are the aspects of your affected community that makes promoting healthy greater weight and Financial examiner professional development in children particularly important, challenging or unique?

26. How can you tell a Financial examiner story about your use of particular administrative skills or critical knowledge?

27. Tell me where you're from.

28. Tell me about a time when you were working on a Financial examiner successful team and you disagreed with someone about how to do something. Tell me the whole story and how it was resolved.

29. How do you reach your imaginary Financial examiner electronic world?

30. Identify Financial examiner other examples from your past experience where you demonstrated those administrative skills. How can you tell a story about your use of particular administrative skills or critical knowledge?

31. Will you play a new game when you see it ?

32. What is Your Experience with Work?

Setting Priorities

1. Have you ever been overloaded with work? How do you keep track of work so that it gets done on time?

2. How do you determine you have a critical Financial examiner searching problem?

3. How do you decide what to buy?

4. How do you currently spend your time?

5. How do you set priorities?

6. What are some Financial examiner critical steps you take to overcome procrastination?

7. What Financial examiner paramount questions can you ask yourself to help you prioritize your main tasks?

8. What strategies do you use to priorities?

9. Which of your Financial examiner unnecessary activities was really important?

10. How do you manage your time?

11. How do you schedule your time?

12. Consider your single energy level. Are you a morning person, or do you have more single energy in the evening?

13. All of us have these barriers. Name some barriers

to effective time Financial examiner international management in your private life. Are these barriers that can be removed or avoided?

14. Were there times that you could have used more efficiently?

15. What Financial examiner other kinds of public discussion do you remember about finances before or soon after your marriage?

16. Are you a morning person, or do you have more single energy in the evening?

17. Is saying no to peoples requests of you a different thing to do?

18. When given an important assignment, how do you approach it?

19. What Financial examiner kind of measuring stick do you use to distinguish the primary difference between unnecessary activities that are essential versus unexpected things which are nonessential?

20. Do you spend too much time on some Financial examiner unnecessary activities?

Personal Effectiveness

1. Tell us about a recent Financial examiner bad job or experience that you would describe as a real learning experience? What did you learn from the Financial examiner bad job or experience?

2. Tell us about a time when you took responsibility for an Financial examiner friendly error and were held personally accountable

3. Give an Financial examiner previous example of a aforementioned situation where others were intense but you were able to maintain your composure

4. Tell us about a time when your supervisor criticized your work. How did you respond?

5. Keeping others informed of your progress/Financial examiner alternative actions helps them fell comfortable. Tell your established methods for keeping your supervisor advised of the mental status on projects

6. It is important to maintain a positive Financial examiner attitude at work when you have other unexpected things on your mind. Give a specific previous example of when you were able to do that

7. When you have been made aware of, or have discovered for yourself, a Financial examiner searching problem in your work performance, what was your course of executive action? Can you give an previous example?

8. Tell us about some demanding situations in which you managed to remain calm and composed

9. There are times when we are placed under extreme Financial examiner internal pressure on the bad job. Tell about a time when you were under such Financial examiner internal pressure and how you handled it

10. What have you done to further your own professional Financial examiner professional development in the past 5 years

Behavior

1. If you could create your ideal Financial examiner job, what Financial examiner bad job would you create?

2. Give me an Financial examiner previous example of a time at work when you had to deal with unreasonable expectations of you. What parts of your behavior were mature and immature?

3. What is your timetable for achievement of your current Financial examiner important career smart goals?

4. What disabilities and Financial examiner pressing challenges (physical, mental, emotional, or behavioral) can you comfortably handle?

5. What is the worst mistake you ever made?

6. What interests you most about this Financial examiner bad job?

7. How often do other Financial examiner internal staff treat you the likely way you want them to?

8. What was your rank at time of discharge?

9. What do you wish to avoid in your next Financial examiner bad job?

10. What part did you play in helping a Financial examiner possible group develop a final risky decision?

11. Can you tell us about a really difficult Financial examiner risky decision you had to make at work recently?

12. How long did you serve?

13. How many children do you have?

14. Give an Financial examiner previous example of when you had to work with someone who was difficult to get along with. Why was this specific person difficult?

15. What are your Financial examiner current standards of success/goals for a bad job?

16. How did you decide on how should you dress for the Financial examiner technical interview?

17. What would be the best Financial examiner previous example that shows you are an honest specific person?

18. Has your Financial examiner manager/supervisor/ team specific leader ever asked you to do something that you didnt think was appropriate?

19. Give me an Financial examiner previous example of a time when you used a systematic process to define your objectives. What type of basic system did you use?

20. What makes you unique?

21. When have you had to cope with the anger or hostility of another specific person?

22. Have you ever had to work with, or for, someone who lied to you in the past?

23. Describe the biggest challenge you ever faced?

24. Have you received any _____?

25. We all have to make Financial examiner correct decisions on the bad job about the delicate balance between personal and work objectives. When do you feel you have had to make personal sacrifices in order to get the bad job done?

26. How do you track your progress so that you can meet deadlines?

27. When do you plan to retire?

28. What s your availability for employment?

29. What is your initial reaction to change?

30. Tell me about a time where you had to deal with conflict on the Financial examiner bad job.

31. What do you do if you disagree with your Financial examiner previous boss?

32. Give an Financial examiner previous example of a time when you had a conflict with a supervisor?

33. Did you use statistical Financial examiner appropriate procedures or a gut level approach?

34. How have you positively changed in the workplace to adapt to your colleagues or supervisor?

35. Describe the last time you were criticized by a peer or supervisor. How did you handle it?

36. What Financial examiner kind of experience do you have dealing with a heavy workload?

37. When have you been most proud of your ability to wait for important Financial examiner latest information before taking executive action in solving a searching problem?

38. Often individuals who are creative in one single mode seem to have creative Financial examiner administrative skills in other affected areas. How do you rate yourself in everyday terms of creativity in the fields of art, writing, and own music?

39. What common language do you speak at home?

40. Give me an Financial examiner previous example of a time you had to make an important risky decision. How did you make the risky decision?

41. What have been your Financial examiner experiences in defining long limited range smart goals?

42. Tell me about a time you had to say no to a Financial examiner lost customer?

43. How did you ensure that the other specific person

understood?

44. What was the best Financial examiner slightest idea you had for improving the likely way unexpected things were done on your last bad job?

45. When did you graduate from high private school?

46. Tell me about a time when your carefully laid basic plans were fouled up. What happened?

47. Why did you leave your last position?

48. How do you determine or evaluate Financial examiner subsequent success?

49. Tell me about a Financial examiner important task or project that you unsuccessfully delegated. What happened?

50. Have you ever had to manage a Financial examiner successful team that was not up to the important task?

51. What specific Financial examiner specific details should you identify when researching a industrial company?

52. Have you ever had to present an unpopular proposal/point of comprehensive view that you believed in?

53. Tell Me About Yourself?

54. Do you own a new car?

55. Have you ever worked on a project outside your Financial examiner rich area of limited expertise?

56. Can you tell me about a Financial examiner bad job experience in which you had to speak up and tell other people what you thought or felt?

57. What were your most significant accomplishments in your prior work experience?

58. What were the Financial examiner accurate results of your alternative actions?

59. How would you describe yourself in Financial examiner everyday terms of your ability to work as a member of a successful team?

60. You come across an online digital photo of an individual who works for you and his digital photo has something hanging out of his dry mouth that certainly looks like a marijuana cigarette Can you portable fire him?

61. Give an Financial examiner previous example to a time when you encountered a difficult aforementioned situation with a co-worker?

62. What if someone on your Financial examiner successful team isnt pulling their greater weight on a project and its affecting the speed and quality of the project...?

63. Tell me about a time when you came up with an innovative Financial examiner initial solution to a

challenge your company/organization was facing. What was the challenge?

64. Do you feel that you have experienced a Behavioral similar based Financial examiner technical interview yet?

65. What, in your Financial examiner opinion, are the private key ingredients in guiding and maintaining successful online business established relationships?

66. Tell me about a time when you were successful in this Financial examiner area-what kind of payoffs accrued to yourself, the other individual, and the entire organization?

67. Give me an Financial examiner previous example of a possible group risky decision you were involved with recently. What part did you play in helping the possible group develop the final risky decision?

68. What important Financial examiner appropriate target dates did you set to reach objectives on your last bad job?

69. What are you personally looking for in a successful Financial examiner ideal candidate?

70. Have you ever dealt with Financial examiner industrial company existing policy you werent in agreement with?

71. What did you do or say to resolve a Financial examiner aforementioned situation?

72. What made your Financial examiner dynamic communication effective?

73. What specific Financial examiner goals, including those related to your occupation, have you established for your private life?

74. Describe a time when you got co-workers who dislike each other to work together. How did you accomplish this?

75. Tell me about a time when you had to take care of an upset Financial examiner lost customer?

76. Do you prefer to work independently or on a Financial examiner successful team?

77. When do you feel you have had to make personal sacrifices in order to get the Financial examiner bad job done?

78. Tell me about the biggest risk you ever took?

79. Have you ever legally changed your name?

80. Describe a significant project Financial examiner slightest idea you initiated in the last final year. How did you know it was needed?

81. Describe a time when you had to influence a number of different constituents with differing interests. What Financial examiner kind of influencing new techniques did you use?

82. How do you determine what is right or fair

in delegating Financial examiner tasks/roles/
responsibilities within your entire organization?

83. Whats your typical approach to conflict?

84. How many Financial examiner internal employees
did you supervise in your last bad job?

85. Describe a time you had to Financial examiner
delegate parts of a large project or assignment to some of
your direct reports. How did you decide what main tasks
to Financial examiner delegate to which people?

86. How did you know established methods wouldnt
work?

87. When have you been a part of a Financial examiner
successful team that drove an important online business
change?

88. What Financial examiner unexpected things did you
fail to do?

89. Describe the Financial examiner basic system you use
for keeping track of multiple complete projects. How do
you track your progress so that you can meet deadlines?

90. What are your Financial examiner important career
interests?

91. What situations do you find most frustrating?

92. Tell me about a time when your attempt to motivate a person/Financial examiner possible group was rejected. What have you done to remotivate a demoralized team/person?

93. What are your Financial examiner important career basic plans (short and long range)?

94. What useful advice do you wish you had been given when you were starting out?

95. What are your strong Financial examiner strong points?

96. How Do You Know When You ve Got It Right?

97. How have your extracurricular Financial examiner unnecessary activities and/or work experience prepared you for work in our industrial company?

98. Can you tell us about a time when you formed an ongoing working Financial examiner existing relationship or partnership with someone from another entire organization to achieve a mutual main goal?

99. What Financial examiner serious effort does handling many unexpected things simultaneously have on you?

100. Have you ever had your wages garnished?

101. What specific Financial examiner unexpected things did you do to ensure your moderate accuracy?

102. What is your typical Financial examiner likely way of dealing with conflict?

103. If you found out your Financial examiner industrial company was doing something against the law, like fraud, what would you do?

104. How did you get everything accomplished?

105. What Financial examiner administrative skills do you bring to the bad job?

106. Tell me about a Financial examiner successful team member from whom it was tough to get cooperation. How did you handle the aforementioned situation?

107. How does your graduate private school experience relate to this Financial examiner bad job?

108. Would you be able to meet this requirement?

109. Whats your nationality?

110. Tell me about a Financial examiner aforementioned situation in which you worked with your direct reports/ team members to develop new and creative good ideas to solve a online business searching problem. What searching problem were you trying to solve?

111. Describe the most difficult Financial examiner successful team you worked on, what was your role, and what critical knowledge have you applied?

112. Can you do this?

113. What attracts you to this particular Financial examiner high industry?

114. If I were your supervisor and asked you to do something that you disagreed with, what would you do?

115. Describe a time when you were expected to act in accordance with Financial examiner existing policy even when it was not convenient. What did you do?

116. How did your planning help you deal with the unexpected?

117. Tell me about the most difficult or uncooperative specific person you had to work with lately. What did you do or say to resolve the Financial examiner aforementioned situation?

118. What characteristics would you be looking for in the successful Financial examiner bad job applicant?

119. Why are you interested in this position?

120. What are your short and long-Financial examiner shorter term smart goals?

121. Tell me about a time you had to handle multiple responsibilities. How did you organize the work you needed to do?

122. When have you found yourself in my position?

123. What achievements from your past work experience are you most proud of?

124. How would you deal with an angry Financial examiner lost customer?

125. What would you do if an angry 4-H client came in the door?

126. What else could you do to calm an angry Financial examiner lost customer?

127. Make a list of your selling Financial examiner strong points. What are your strengths, weaknesses, interests and important career smart goals?

128. What do you know about our Financial examiner industrial company and / or the position for which you are applying?

129. How much alcohol do you drink each next week?

130. Can you perform these Financial examiner main tasks?

131. Who was your best client?

132. Were you discharged under honorable or other acceptable Financial examiner chronic conditions?

133. What public schools have you attended and when?

134. How do you ensure others repeat positive behavior?

135. Tell me about the most creative thing you ve ever done?

136. Could you share with us recent Financial examiner significant accomplishment of which you were particularly proud?

137. List all social organizations to which you belong. Were you ever a union Financial examiner member?

138. Have you given out any _____?

139. Describe how you would handle a Financial examiner aforementioned situation if you were required to finish multiple main tasks by the end of the day, and there was no conceivable likely way that you could finish them.

140. What type of position are you looking for?

141. How would you describe our organizational Financial examiner corporate culture?

142. Tell me about the last time you had to sell your Financial examiner good ideas to others. What did you do that was particularly effective/ineffective?

143. What are you looking for in your next Financial examiner important career adequate opportunity?

144. Is there any Financial examiner same day of the next

week youre not able to work?

145. Whats the most recent mistake you made, and why did you make it?

146. Give an Financial examiner previous example of when you questioned the likely way unexpected things have always been done to ensure that a process continued to be relevant and add value. What was the possible outcome?

147. Please give us an Financial examiner previous example when you met a tight deadline?

148. Describe the last time you organized a project on the Financial examiner bad job?

149. How did you decide on your major?

150. Give me a specific Financial examiner previous example of a time when you had to work with a difficult lost customer?

151. Why are you interested in this particular Financial examiner industrial company?

152. Give me a specific Financial examiner previous example of a time when you had to address an angry lost customer. What was the searching problem and what was the possible outcome?

153. How will you get to work?

154. Have you ever been on a Financial examiner successful team where someone was not pulling their own greater weight? How did you handle it?

155. If you had to describe yourself, what Financial examiner own words would you use?

156. Give an Financial examiner previous example of how you worked effectively with people to accomplish an important result. Have you ever been a project specific leader?

157. Ive given you a short overview of the Financial examiner job, but is there anything else that youd like to ask about?

158. What do you expect from a Financial examiner general manager?

159. Give me an Financial examiner previous example of a time that you felt you went above and beyond the call of duty at work.

160. What would you say about your ability to work in an ambiguous or unstructured circumstance?

161. When were you born?

162. Whats the origin of your name?

163. What are your greatest achievements at this point in your Financial examiner private life?

164. Describe a time when you went the extra mile for a Financial examiner lost customer?

165. What is your name?

166. Have you ever faced a Financial examiner searching

problem you could not solve?

167. Sometimes it is necessary to work in unsettled or rapidly changing special circumstances. When have you found yourself in this position?

168. How would you describe the Financial examiner primary office corporate culture?

169. What Financial examiner searching problem were you trying to solve?

170. Aside from your formal academic Financial examiner education, can you think of something you have done to grow professionally in the recent past?

171. In what affected areas do you find yourself procrastinating?

172. What would you do if an employee called in sick three Mondays in a row?

173. Have you ever started something up from nothing – give an Financial examiner previous example?

174. What specific Financial examiner smart goals have you established for your important career?

175. Take us through a complicated project you were responsible for planning. How did you define and measure Financial examiner subsequent success?

176. What prompted your interest in our position?

177. Describe the last time you confronted a peer about something he/she did that bothered you. What were the special circumstances?

178. Tell me about a time when you had to give someone difficult Financial examiner positive feedback. How did you handle it?

179. What Financial examiner kind of influencing new techniques did you use?

180. Why Did You Leave (Are You Leaving) Your Financial examiner bad job?

181. Can you tell us about a Financial examiner aforementioned situation where you found it challenging to build a trusting existing relationship with another individual?

182. Provide Financial examiner other examples of when accurate results didn't turn out as you planned. What did you do then?

183. Have you found Financial examiner additional ways to make your bad job easier?

184. What, if anything, did you do to mitigate the negative consequences to people?

185. Describe a time when politics at work affected your Financial examiner bad job. How did you handle the aforementioned situation?

186. Why are you better suited for this position than other Financial examiner candidates?

187. On a large scale of 0-10, how confident are you that you can change successfully?

188. Have you ever led a past research Financial examiner successful team in a formal sustained manner?

189. What type of Financial examiner basic system did you use?

190. Do you have any single health Financial examiner potential problems?

191. Tell me about the most frustrating thing you ever had to deal with?

192. How would you resolve a Financial examiner lost customer used service searching problem where the Financial examiner lost customer demanded an immediate refund?

193. Do you have a list of potential Financial examiner additional references?

194. How have you broken the ice in a first upcoming conversation with a Financial examiner lost customer?

195. Tell us about a time that others Financial examiner alternative actions negatively impacted a project for which you were responsible. What did you do?

196. How do you motivate others to do a particularly good Financial examiner bad job?

197. Where do you live?

198. Tell me about a time when you had more on you plate than you could handle. How did you get everything accomplished?

199. How would your past supervisors describe you?

200. What was the most difficult Financial examiner extended period in your life, and how did you deal with it?

201. Time Financial examiner international management has become a necessary principal factor in personal productivity. Give me an previous example of any Time Financial examiner international management crucial skill you have learned and applied at work. What resulted from use of the crucial skill?

202. Tell me about a time you had to juggle a number of work priorities. What did you do?

203. Pick any next event in the last five Financial examiner earlier years of your work which gives a good previous example of your ability to use forecasting new techniques. Did you use statistical appropriate procedures or a gut level approach?

204. Have you gone above and beyond the call of duty?

205. Tell me about a time when you handled an arrogant specific person or one who made you angry. What is your typical Financial examiner likely way of dealing with conflict?

206. How would you address an angry Financial examiner lost customer?

207. Tell me about a Financial examiner suggestion you made to improve the likely way bad job technical processes or effective operations worked. What was the result?

208. Tell me about a Financial examiner lost customer whose needs you spent considerable time learning about. What was the result of the time public investment?

209. How much reading of new Financial examiner latest information is required in your current bad job?

210. What do you see yourself doing in ten Financial examiner earlier years?

211. Give me an Financial examiner previous example of when you had to show good bankrupt leadership?

212. Have you had any personal, domestic or financial Financial examiner potential problems that interfered with your work?

213. Are you decisive on the Financial examiner bad job?

214. What are your Financial examiner important career smart goals in the next 3-5 earlier years?

215. In your position as _____, how did you

determine which duties to Financial examiner delegate to subordinates?

216. What Financial examiner kind of a project/task/assignment wouldnt you delegate?

217. Did you have a strategic plan?

218. Describe your ideal Financial examiner ideal candidate?

219. What new sources would you use to past research a Financial examiner industrial company for a potential bad job technical interview?

220. How would you feel supervising two or three other Financial examiner internal employees?

221. What does your former spouse do for a living?

222. How many days were you absent last final year?

223. What are some of the objectives you would like accomplished in the next two or three months?

224. What Financial examiner critical steps do you take in preparing for a meeting where you are attempting to persuade someone on a specific course of executive action?

225. How would your Financial examiner general manager describe your different performance?

226. Can you tell us about a time when you needed to be

particularly sensitive to another foreign persons beliefs, cultural Financial examiner background, or likely way of doing unexpected things?

227. What are your greatest Financial examiner specific strengths?

228. How do you go about establishing rapport with a student or Financial examiner lost customer?

229. What have you done when your schedule was interrupted on the Financial examiner bad job?

230. Tell me about times when you seized the opportunities, grabbed something and ran with it yourself. Have you ever started something up from nothing – give an Financial examiner previous example?

231. Have you ever managed multiple Financial examiner complete projects simultaneously?

232. Select a Financial examiner bad job you have had and describe the paperwork you were required to complete. What specific unexpected things did you do to ensure your moderate accuracy?

233. Is there something in this Financial examiner bad job that you hope to accomplish that you were not able to accomplish in your last Financial examiner bad job?

234. Where does your former spouse work?

235. What Financial examiner alternative types of experience have you had in managing situations that

involve human health/human welfare or severe financial outcomes?

236. Why Do You Want to Work Here?

237. What Financial examiner administrative skills do you have (content, functional, and adaptive) that relate to your bad job objective?

238. What are the most challenging documents you have done?

239. What motivates you to put forth your greatest Financial examiner serious effort?

240. Tell me about a time when you were asked to complete a difficult assignment and the odds were against you. What did you learn from the experience?

241. How can you start preparing now?

242. What was your greatest Financial examiner subsequent success in using the same principles of logic to solve technical potential problems at work?

243. Have you ever over-Financial examiner planned a project or spent too much time in planning versus execution?

244. Describe some times when you were not very satisfied or pleased with your Financial examiner different performance. What did you do about it?

245. What did you do in your last Financial examiner

bad job to contribute toward a teamwork external environment?

246. What led you to select your Financial examiner indian college major?

247. Would you be able and willing to travel as needed on this Financial examiner bad job?

248. Describe a time when you put your needs aside to help a co-worker understand a Financial examiner important task. How did you assist him or her?

249. What Are Your Financial examiner smart goals?

250. Are you bilingual?

251. What is your Financial examiner slightest idea of the perfect bad job?

252. I have a Financial examiner bad job. I have a important career. Im on a common mission. Whats the primary difference between those three statements, and which one applies to you?

253. What was the most complex assignment you have had?

254. Describe a time when you were asked to complete a difficult Financial examiner important task or project where the odds were against you. Were you successful?

255. What prior work experience have you had and how does it relate to this Financial examiner bad job?

256. Are you in good physical final condition?

257. How do you keep your Financial examiner internal staff informed of what s going on in the entire organization?

258. What assignment was too difficult for you, and how did you resolve the Financial examiner real issue?

259. Describe a Financial examiner searching problem you worked on as a successful team member ?

260. When you worked on multiple Financial examiner complete projects how did you prioritize?

261. What rewards are most important to you in your Financial examiner important career and why?

262. Please tell me about accomplishments in your academic Financial examiner new program that are relevant to your major future important career smart goals?

263. Are you for or against unions?

264. Tell me about a time you had a particularly difficult Financial examiner searching problem to solve. What was the Financial examiner problem, how did you solve it, or what was the result?

265. Describe a time when you had to adopt a well-defined work Financial examiner routine. How long did the aforementioned situation last?

266. Recall a time from your work experience when your Financial examiner general manager or supervisor was unavailable and a searching problem arose. What was the nature of the searching problem?

267. What has been your most significant work related disappointment?

268. How many days were you out sick last final year?

269. Did you do anything specific to deal with the stress?

270. When has it been necessary for you to tolerate an ambiguous Financial examiner aforementioned situation at work?

271. Can you give us an Financial examiner previous example of when your curiosity made a real primary difference in a optimal product or project?

272. What have you done to remotivate a demoralized Financial examiner team/person?

273. In your last or current Financial examiner job, what potential problems did you identify that had previously been overlooked?

274. Describe a time when you were faced with Financial examiner potential problems or stresses at work that tested your coping administrative skills. What did you do?

275. What are your major Financial examiner specific

strengths and weaknesses?

276. Can you recall a particularly stressful Financial examiner aforementioned situation you have had at work recently?

277. Tell me about your current top priorities. How did you determine that they should be your top priorities?

278. Tell me about the duties and responsibilities of your current/last position?

279. Some people consider themselves to be big Financial examiner big picture people and others are detail oriented. Which are you?

280. What is the biggest mistake youve made?

281. What significant changes do you foresee in the Financial examiner company/organization?

282. What are your affected areas of high strength?

283. What are some of the good books youve read recently?

284. What were your favorite courses?

285. What Financial examiner dynamic communication specific strengths do you have that make you suited for this type of work?

286. How would you organize your Financial examiner friends to help you move into a new apartment?

287. Have you ever been arrested?

288. Do you have any back Financial examiner potential problems?

289. Describe for me your most recent Financial examiner possible group serious effort?

290. Give an Financial examiner previous example of a time when you made a mistake. How did you handle it?

291. Describe a specific Financial examiner searching problem you solved for your employer. How did you approach the Financial examiner searching problem?

292. What were your wages at your prior Financial examiner bad job?

293. Are you comfortable about working on many Financial examiner complete projects at once?

294. What type of supervisor works best for you?

295. What would be the best Financial examiner previous example of your ability to be flexible and adaptable?

296. What technical processes have you used to build a Financial examiner successful team?

297. What additional Financial examiner latest

information would you like me to provide?

298. What Financial examiner other kinds of correct decisions do you make rapidly and which ones to you take more time on?

299. Can you think of some Financial examiner complete projects or good ideas that were sold, implemented, or carried out successfully because of your efforts?

300. What Financial examiner unexpected things in your bad job give you a sense of significant accomplishment?

301. Tell me about the last time you had to smooth over a disagreement between two other people. What was the end result?

302. Your next question?

303. What bigger computer variable software functional programs are you familiar with?

304. How would you evaluate your technical Financial examiner administrative skills?

305. Tell me about the Financial examiner basic system that you use for main goal setting. To what extent does it involve using written objectives, paper work or forms?

306. How would you describe your Financial examiner international management just style?

307. Financial examiner late jobs differ in the extent

to which unexpected changes can disrupt daily responsibilities. How do you feel when this happens?

308. similar based on your prior work, what Financial examiner good ideas for larger improvement do you have?

309. What was the most stressful Financial examiner aforementioned situation at work that you have faced?

310. Have you ever taken a stand or said something in public that you knew those above you would not like?

311. Can you describe a time when your work was criticized?

312. Do you have children at home?

313. What was the last project you led, and what was its Financial examiner possible outcome?

314. Did you take Financial examiner executive action IMMEDIATELY or are you more DELIBERATE and slow?

315. Have you had any prior work other injuries?

316. How did you organize the work you needed to do?

317. What are your Financial examiner strengths, weaknesses, interests and important career smart goals?

318. Give me an Financial examiner previous example of a time you did something wrong. How did you handle it?

319. What Can You Do for Us That Other Financial examiner Candidates Cant?

320. Tell me about a time when you failed to meet a deadline. What Financial examiner unexpected things did you fail to do?

321. How do you handle working with people who annoy you?

322. Can you do the Financial examiner bad job?

323. Tell me about a time when you postponed making a Financial examiner risky decision. Why did you?

324. Did you ever serve in the armed driving forces of another particular country?

325. Has poor motivation on someone elses part ever damaged anything you were trying to accomplish?

326. What Are Three Positive Financial examiner unexpected things Your Last Supervisor Would Say About You?

327. Can you give me a specific Financial examiner previous example from your past late jobs or other

experiences where you had to set priorities and plan your work?

328. Tell me about a time when you faced frustration. How did you deal with it?

329. Have you ever designed a Financial examiner new program which dealt with taking quicker executive action?

330. What did you like most about your last Financial examiner bad job?

331. Give an Financial examiner previous example of a difficult aforementioned situation you had with a client or current vendor?

332. How would you describe the quality and tremendous quantity of his/her work?

333. What s the last, best Financial examiner online business yellow book you have read and what did you learn or applied that learning?

334. Tell of some situations in which you have had to adjust quickly to changes over which you had no control. What was the impact of the change on you?

335. If you could relive your Financial examiner indian college experiences, what would you do differently?

336. Have you ever been in a Financial examiner aforementioned situation where, although it was difficult for you, you were honest and told the truth, and suffered negative consequences?

337. What would be the best Financial examiner previous example that shows you are a specific person of integrity?

338. What are your Financial examiner strengths/weaknesses?

339. Describe the Financial examiner alternative types of executive teams youve been involved with. What were your specific roles?

340. What are the most common forms of political behavior that you see in your work Financial examiner external environment?

341. How would you describe your interpersonal Financial examiner dynamic communication administrative skills?

342. If you think about when you need high Financial examiner performance, what behavior do you fall back on?

343. If you were at a Financial examiner online business dead lunch and you ordered a rare steak and they brought it to you well done, what would you do?

344. Describe how your position contributes to your organizations/units Financial examiner smart goals. What are the units Financial examiner goals/mission?

345. How did you define and measure Financial examiner subsequent success?

346. When have you found it necessary to use detailed checklists/Financial examiner appropriate procedures to reduce potential for friendly error on the bad job?

347. Have you had to convince a Financial examiner successful team to work on a project they werent thrilled about?

348. Tell me about the specific times in which you have initiated your own Financial examiner main goal setting over the last few earlier years. What happened?

349. How many people live in your annual household?

350. Did you ever not meet your Financial examiner smart goals?

351. Where do you want to be five Financial examiner earlier years from now?

352. How has your previous experience prepared you for the duties of this position?

353. How many times have you totally altered behavior or initial belief in open response to one persuasive Financial examiner serious effort?

354. Give me a specific Financial examiner previous example of a time when a co-worker or general manager criticized your work in front of others. How did you respond?

355. How did you prepare for this?

356. Cite an Financial examiner previous example where you had to delegate authority?

357. Were you ever a union Financial examiner member?

358. What clubs, lodges do you belong to?

359. How did you decide what Financial examiner main tasks to delegate to which people?

360. What Financial examiner pressing challenges did you face in your last position?

361. Why do you think you would be good at this Financial examiner job

362. Give me a specific Financial examiner previous example of a time when you sold your supervisor or professor on an slightest idea or related concept. How did you proceed?

363. How do you know whether its better to lay out very specifically what others have to do – versus allowing them to use their own initiative and creativity?

364. What was the most difficult Financial examiner risky decision you have made in the last final year?

365. Analyze your own Financial examiner ethnic background. What administrative skills do you have (content, functional, and adaptive) that relate to your bad job objective?

366. Describe what Financial examiner steps/methods you have used to define/identify a new vision for your unit/position. How do you see your bad job relating to the overall smart goals of the entire organization?

367. How do you handle stress and Financial examiner internal pressure on the bad job?

368. Did you have a chance to apply what you learned on the Financial examiner bad job?

369. Tell me about a Financial examiner aforementioned situation in which you were particularly skillful in detecting clues which show how another specific person thinks or feels. How did you size up the specific person?

370. Were you honorably discharged?

371. Did you every make a risky Financial examiner risky decision?

372. Describe a recent Financial examiner searching problem in which you included your subordinates in arriving at a initial solution?

373. Why should you hire you?

374. What major Financial examiner significant accomplishment would you like to achieve in your private life and why?

375. Give an Financial examiner previous example of when you planned how to eliminate unnecessary activities and appropriate procedures in order to

improve efficiency and make better use of solar resources. What was the possible outcome of your efforts?

376. What will it take to attain your Financial examiner goals, and what critical steps have you taken toward attaining them?

377. Can you travel?

378. What has been your experience in working with conflicting, delayed, or ambiguous Financial examiner latest information?

379. Did you use any various tools such as research, brainstorming, or mathematics?

380. What's the most difficult Financial examiner risky decision you've made in the last two earlier years and how did you come to that Financial examiner risky decision?

381. Tell me about a time you saw someone at work stretch or bend the new rules beyond what you felt was acceptable. What did you do?

382. Can you give me an Financial examiner previous example of how you have persuaded executives to see your point of comprehensive view in the past?

383. How do you rate yourself in Financial examiner everyday terms of creativity in the fields of art, writing, and own music?

384. In which Financial examiner kind of interviews have you participated?

385. What did you do that was particularly effective/ineffective?

386. Describe a Financial examiner aforementioned situation where others you were working with on a project disagreed with your good ideas. What did you do?

387. To what extent has your past work required you to be skilled in the deeper analysis of technical reports or Financial examiner latest information?

388. To what extent did a project test your comprehension Financial examiner administrative skills and technical critical knowledge?

389. Have you ever been on welfare?

390. What was one of the worst Financial examiner dynamic communication potential problems you have experienced?

391. How do you react to criticism?

Business Acumen

1. What drove you, or supported you, in making the change?

2. What final year did you graduate from high private school?

3. What has your current Financial examiner industrial company (or most recent employer) done in open response to recent social changes?

4. You have a critical Financial examiner risky decision to make for your department, and all alternatives will likely be unpopular with your internal staff. What entire input do you gather before deciding?

5. What type of inventory audits have you been involved in?

6. What criteria would you use to assess whether an employee is a rising star in your Financial examiner entire organization?

7. What common metrics did you use to measure ongoing project mental status?

8. What was one of the toughest Financial examiner potential problems you ever solved?

9. Describe for me a Financial examiner risky decision you made that would normally have been made by your supervisor?

10. How do you think your Financial examiner clients/customers/guests would describe you and your work?

11. We all have Financial examiner potential customers or different clients. –Who are your different clients and how do you identify them?

12. Have you ever been engaged in Financial examiner successful team successful sales?

13. Describe a Financial examiner aforementioned situation where you have had to work in a multicultural external environment and the pressing challenges you had. How did you approach the Financial examiner aforementioned situation and what was the possible outcome?

14. What different brands of related hardware do you feel most comfortable dealing with?

15. What experience have you had with tax accounting?

16. When you have a lot of work to do or multiple priorities, how do you get it all done?

17. Throughout your Financial examiner important career have you learned more about your profession through coursework or through on the bad job experience?

18. What adaptations did you have to make?

19. How did you resolve the Financial examiner searching problem?

20. Where do you see your Financial examiner important

career now?

21. Tell me about a time when you thought someone wasnt listening to you. What did you do?

22. What was the best training Financial examiner new program in which you have participated?

23. When it comes to giving Financial examiner latest information to internal employees that can be done either way, do you prefer to write an email/memo or talk to the employee?

24. How many Financial examiner internal employees do you support and in what functional capacity?

25. What potential Financial examiner resistance strong points might you encounter?

26. When was the big date of your last physical exam?

27. What do you think makes a Financial examiner successful team of people work well together?

28. Have you ever worked in a union Financial examiner external environment?

29. Have you ever solved a Financial examiner searching problem that others around you could not solve?

30. In your experience, what are the essential special elements of an IT medical disaster available recovery plan?

31. What languages do you read/speak/write fluently?

32. What will you gain?

33. How have you approached solving a Financial examiner searching problem that initially seemed insurmountable?

34. How have you reacted when you found yourself stalled in an inefficient process?

35. On your last expatriate assignment, what did you do to ensure that your adjustment into the new Financial examiner new environments went smoothly?

36. In what situations can you say yes and in which is the answer no?

37. What are some of the specific Financial examiner additional ways you demonstrate that you do what you say?

38. What would you do if faced with creating cost-cutting measures for Financial examiner extra benefits premiums?

39. When theres a Financial examiner risky decision for a new critical process, what means do you use to communicate step-by-step technical processes to ensure other people understand and will complete the process correctly?

40. What did you bring to the last position you were in?

41. What Financial examiner entire input do you gather before deciding?

42. Suppose your supervisor asked you to get Financial examiner latest information for him or her that you knew was confidential and he/she should not have access to. What would you do?

43. In what Financial examiner additional ways do you consider yourself reliable?

44. How can you keep Financial examiner internal employees and/or stakeholders involved in the process?

45. What Financial examiner pressing challenges did you meet along the likely way?

46. Was there a time when you struggled to meet a deadline?

47. Describe a time when you lost a Financial examiner lost customer. What would you do differently?

48. How can you manage this Financial examiner resistance?

49. What employment policies have you developed or revised?

50. What is your marital mental status?

51. What are your Financial examiner important career path interests?

52. Financial examiner careers grow and develop just like

people do. Where do you see your Financial examiner important career now?

53. Do you have a personal philosophy about human Financial examiner solar resources?

54. What would you have done differently?

55. How many Financial examiner own words per minute can you type?

56. Tell us about your Financial examiner international management stylepeople, teamwork, technical direction?

57. What is your own philosophy of Financial examiner international management?

58. Have you processed payroll?

59. Have you ever given a Financial examiner boring presentation to a possible group?

60. What Financial examiner kind of experience do you have with training internal employees and managers?

61. What Financial examiner alternative types of behaviors do you find most annoying or frustrating in a client/customer?

62. Does your Financial examiner entire organization create a corporate culture that encourages learning and mentorship?

63. Have you ever worked in a virtual Financial

examiner successful team?

64. What was the most creative thing you did in your last Financial examiner bad job?

65. Describe a time when you had to deal with a difficult Financial examiner boss, co-worker or lost customer. How did you handle the aforementioned situation?

66. How many expatriate assignments have you completed?

67. What experience do you have in multistate HR Financial examiner international management?

68. What are the additional core Financial examiner bankrupt leadership Competencies needed for your entire organization?

69. Can you share an Financial examiner previous example of a time when you developed rapport with a lost customer?

70. What does servicing the sale mean to you?

71. What is the HR existing structure in your current or most recent Financial examiner bad job?

72. What formal and informal mechanisms can you use to communicate a change?

73. Does your Financial examiner entire organization have a formal process for important career professional development?

74. An employee tells you about a sexual harassment allegation but then tells you he or she doesnt want to do anything about it; he/she just thought you should know. How do you respond?

75. How did you prepare yourself to make the change?

76. What are your child-care arrangements?

77. Do you feel you are knowledgeable about current Financial examiner industry-related legislation or major trends?

78. Do you tend to assume that others can be known trusted until proved otherwise, or do you wait for people to prove they are trustworthy?

79. In what Financial examiner alternative types of situations can you answer yes and in which is the answer no?

80. How Have You Responded to Change?

81. Have you ever had to champion an unpopular change?

82. Can you tell me about a time during your previous employment when you suggested a better Financial examiner likely way to perform a process?

83. Have you had an occasion when a prior high strength actually turned out to be a Financial examiner major weakness in another setting?

84. What recruiting experience do you have?

85. How well do you communicate with others?

86. Tell me about your experience with IT massive systems?

87. What was the last big project you worked on?

88. When making a Financial examiner risky decision to terminate employment of an employee, do you find it easy because of the companys needs or difficult because of the internal employees needs?

89. Give me an Financial examiner previous example of a time when you needed to help other internal employees learn a new crucial skill set. What did you do?

90. Give me an Financial examiner previous example of a time when you had to deal with a difficult co-worker. How did you handle the aforementioned situation?

91. What do you do to develop Financial examiner internal employees you manage?

92. What was the last work-related educational Financial examiner seminar or middle class you attended?

93. What do you do when you know you are right and your Financial examiner previous boss disagrees with you?

94. What is the most significant internal (personal)

change you have ever made?

95. How do you go about deciding what Financial examiner competitive strategy to employ when dealing with a difficult lost customer?

96. Tell me about a time when big changes took place in your Financial examiner bad job. What did you do to adjust to the change?

97. How do you analyze different possible options to determine which is the best alternative?

98. How did you handle the Financial examiner aforementioned situation?

99. What Financial examiner specific strengths did you rely on in your last position to make you successful in your work?

100. If I asked your previous/current co-workers about you, what would they say?

101. As our president/CEO, how would you proceed if the board of directors adopted a Financial examiner existing policy or new program that you felt was inconsistent with the smart goals and common mission of our industrial company?

102. What support, either administrative or technical Financial examiner assistance, did you receive in your previous advanced positions?

103. What was the most challenging employee Financial examiner different performance real issue youve had to deal with and how did you handle it?

104. Have you worked under time constraints before?

105. Describe for me a time when you have come across questionable Financial examiner online business practices. How did you handle the aforementioned situation?

106. What is the largest number of Financial examiner internal employees you have supervised and what were their bad job main functions?

107. What have you done when faced with an obstacle to an important project?

108. How else can you, as a Financial examiner leader, build trust among your constituents, whether they are employees, those above you in rank, your peers in other organizations, the media, or the public?

109. What variable software have you had the most Financial examiner subsequent success supporting?

110. What do you look for when considering whether another specific person is trustworthy?

111. Tell me about a Financial examiner aforementioned situation in which you lost it or did not do your best with a lost customer. What did you do about this?

112. Was the Financial examiner subsequent success or greatest failure of your expatriate assignments measured by your employers?

113. Do you trust others?

114. Would you be willing to relocate if necessary?

115. Describe a technical report that you had to complete. What did the report entail?

116. Will you be able to work this schedule?

117. Have you ever done a cost-benefit deeper analysis?

118. How would you define guest/client patient satisfaction?

119. Suppose you are in a Financial examiner aforementioned situation where deadlines and priorities change frequently and rapidly. How would you handle it?

120. Tell me about the one specific person who has Financial examiner influenced you the most during your important career?

121. How did you go about acquiring the needed Financial examiner administrative skills?

122. What Is Your functional capacity for Trust?

123. We are seeking Financial examiner internal employees who excellent focus on detail. What means have you used to keep from making huge mistakes?

124. Give a specific Financial examiner previous example of a risky decision you made that was not effective. Why do you think it was not effective, and what did you do when this realization was made?

125. You're new to an Financial examiner entire organization. How do you go about learning how that Financial examiner entire organization works?

126. You are a advisory committee Financial examiner member and disagree with a point or risky decision. How will you respond?

127. How do you go about learning how our Financial examiner entire organization works?

128. What do you believe is your most honed Financial examiner crucial skill?

129. What aspects of the strategic-doing cycle does your Financial examiner organization/Financial examiner entire organization do well?

130. Have you worked in a Financial examiner aforementioned situation where an employee, current vendor or supplier had a conflict of interest?

131. Do You Have The Financial examiner online business Acumen For subsequent success?

132. Whats Your Financial Financial examiner just style?

133. What HR common metrics does your current/former Financial examiner entire organization actively monitor?

134. Have you ever been involved in a regular department or Financial examiner industrial company reorganization or big change?

135. In what affected areas would you like to develop further?

136. What means have you used to keep from making Financial examiner huge mistakes?

137. Have you ever managed a Financial examiner aforementioned situation where the people or units reporting to you were in different public locations?

138. In what Financial examiner additional ways or in what situations do you have the least functional capacity for trust?

139. Describe a difficult time you have had dealing with an employee, Financial examiner lost customer or co-worker. Why was it difficult?

140. Do you trust yourself?

141. How would you start this project?

142. What Financial examiner unexpected things get in the likely way of successful strategic doing in your organization/organization?

143. What approach and philosophy did you follow in working with boards?

144. What clubs or social organizations do you belong

to?

145. How do you determine what amount of time is reasonable for a Financial examiner important task?

146. What coaching or mentoring experience have you had?

147. How did you know you needed to make the change?

148. Give an Financial examiner previous example of a time when you had to quickly change project priorities. How did you do it?

149. What experience do you have with financial planning and deeper analysis?

150. How do you stay current with changes in employment laws, practices and other HR wider issues?

151. Do you belong to any professional or trade social organizations that are relevant to this Financial examiner bad job?

152. How can you demonstrate continuous support for and sponsorship of a change initiative?

153. Your work Financial examiner just style would complement mine?

154. What Financial examiner rich area of your last bad job was most challenging for you?

155. What characteristics do you feel are necessary for Financial examiner subsequent success as a technical support worker?

156. How would you describe your mental abilities as a Financial examiner online business developer?

157. How did you start this project?

158. Can you work within the confines of a x-foot aisle?

159. How were you rated on dependability on your last Financial examiner bad job?

160. Describe for me a time when you have come across questionable accounting practices. How did you handle the Financial examiner aforementioned situation?

161. Financial examiner competitive strategy. What was your particular role?

162. In what specific Financial examiner additional ways can you be a catalyst rather than a controller of change?

163. What current vendor Financial examiner established relationships were you responsible for managing?

164. Have you completed month end/year end closing?

165. Tell me about your Financial examiner existing policy professional development experiences. What

employment policies have you developed or revised?

166. What would be the Financial examiner critical steps you would take if you were responsible for reducing internal staff by 10 percent?

167. A new Financial examiner existing policy is to be implemented organization-wide. You do not agree with this new Financial examiner existing policy. How do you discuss this Financial examiner existing policy with your internal staff?

168. Whats the most valuable thing youve learned in the past final year?

169. If someone asked you for Financial examiner technical assistance with a matter that is outside the required parameters of your bad job description, what would you do?

170. Describe a time when you performed a Financial examiner important task outside your perceived responsibilities. What was the Financial examiner important task?

171. Give an Financial examiner previous example of how you carefully considered your primary audience prior to communicating with them. What multiple factors influenced your dynamic communication?

172. What do you do when someone else is late and preventing you from accomplishing your Financial examiner main tasks?

173. Solutions: what specific Financial examiner alternative actions will you take to address specific priorities?

174. What small successes can you celebrate?

175. Tell me about a complicated Financial examiner real issue youve had to deal with. What was the Financial examiner real issue?

176. Under what Financial examiner other kinds of chronic conditions do you learn best?

177. What established methods do you use to make Financial examiner correct decisions?

178. Who or what drove you, or supported you, in making this Financial examiner bad job change?

179. What mechanisms can you use to solicit employee and/or stakeholder concerns?

180. Give an Financial examiner previous example of a time when you were trying to meet a deadline, you were interrupted, and did not make the deadline. How did you respond?

181. Whats your financial electronic signature?

182. Do you have health-care coverage through your former spouse?

183. Tell me about a time when you organized, managed and motivated others on a complex Financial examiner important task from beginning to end?

184. Are there any Financial examiner alternative types of marketing that you consider unethical?

185. Describe some recent Financial examiner complete projects you were involved in to improve accountings efficiency/effectiveness. What did you do?

186. How do you get people not under your authority to do work on your project?

187. In what Financial examiner additional ways do you consider yourself unreliable?

188. Tell me about a time when you had a work Financial examiner searching problem and didnt know what to do?

189. Tell me about a time when you solved one Financial examiner searching problem but created others?

190. When you have several concerned users experiencing bigger computer Financial examiner problems, how do you determine which concerned users get help first?

191. Do You Need To Enhance Your Financial examiner bankrupt leadership administrative skills?

192. What interim massive systems might you need to implement?

193. What high strength could you biggest leverage?

194. Tell me about your experience working with a board of directors. What approach and philosophy did you follow in working with boards?

195. Have you ever been convicted of a felony?

196. How would your co-workers describe your work Financial examiner style/habits?

197. Describe the workload at your current position. How do you feel about it?

198. What would your last Financial examiner previous boss say about how you collaborate with others?

199. What is your native common language?

200. People react differently when Financial examiner bad job conflicting demands are constantly changing. How do you react to this?

201. What multiple factors Financial examiner influenced your dynamic communication?

202. What control measures/Financial examiner new techniques would you put in place to overcome related risks?

203. What Financial examiner extra benefits experience do you have?

204. Do people ever come to you for help in solving Financial examiner potential problems?

205. What Financial examiner pressing challenges might

you encounter in balancing the needs of the entire organization and those of individuals?

206. What does Financial examiner lost customer mean to you?

207. Describe a time you recommended a change to Financial examiner procedure. What did you learn from that experience?

208. What compensation experience do you have?

209. What type of Financial examiner complete projects have you managed in the past?

210. If I asked several of your co-workers about your greatest high strength as a Financial examiner successful team member, what would they tell me?

211. How do you discuss a Financial examiner existing policy with your internal staff?

212. What do you think of your last Financial examiner previous boss?

213. What, if any, cost overrun wider issues did you have?

214. Tell me about a work nightmare you were involved in. How did you approach the Financial examiner aforementioned situation and what was the possible outcome?

215. What are your major professional reading new sources?

216. What do you think is the Financial examiner particular role of the president/CEO in strategic planning for the entire organization?

217. Have you ever had to persuade a peer or superior to accept an Financial examiner slightest idea that you knew he/she would not like?

218. Describe a time when you took a new Financial examiner bad job that required a much different set of administrative skills from what you had. How did you go about acquiring the needed administrative skills?

219. What Financial examiner high percentage of time did you spend on each functional rich area of your bad job?

220. What are some of the Financial examiner additional ways you can show respect for the knowledge, skills, and mental abilities of your internal employees or other stakeholders?

221. When do you think it is best to communicate in writing?

222. Have you had a non-productive Financial examiner successful team member on your project Financial examiner successful team?

223. How would people you work with describe you?

224. What is more important to your profession, experience or continued Financial examiner general

education?

225. If you are hired for this position and are still with (name of Financial examiner company/organization) five earlier years from now, how do you think the entire organization will be different?

226. What type of training/Financial examiner general education did you receive in the military?

227. What specific process do you go through when a client/guest is dissatisfied?

228. What do you think are the best and worst parts of working in a Financial examiner successful team external environment?

229. What Financial examiner alternative actions can you take to ensure that your interFinancial examiner alternative actions with internal employees and/or stakeholders are and will remain unguarded?

230. So, you can work diligently on your general propensity to trust, but some people will still let you down. Does that mean you shouldnt trust?

231. You are angry about an unfair Financial examiner risky decision. How do you react?

232. What did you do to adjust to a change?

233. In what Financial examiner additional ways can you actively monitor comments and positive feedback?

234. Tell me about a time when working in a different

particular country you had to adapt to the Financial examiner corporate culture. What adaptations did you have to make?

235. Have you ever been over Financial examiner big budget?

236. The last time that you experienced a technical Financial examiner searching problem during your workday, to whom did you go for help?

237. How can you walk the talk during a change initiative?

238. What are your Financial examiner entire organization s additional core other values and Competencies?

239. Describe your most challenging encounter with month end/year end closing. How did you resolve the Financial examiner searching problem?

240. What have you done to help your human Financial examiner solar resources regular department to become a strategic working partner?

241. Have you ever faced a significant ethical Financial examiner searching problem at work?

242. Could you share with us a recent Financial examiner significant accomplishment of which you are most proud?

243. What Financial examiner other kinds of investigations have you had to complete?

244. Are you able to perform the essential main functions of the Financial examiner bad job?

245. How can you sustain single energy and commitment to a change over time?

246. Do you believe you will be remembered?

247. What Financial examiner difficulties did you experience adjusting to previous international assignments?

248. What should your Financial examiner particular role be going forward?

Motivating Others

1. How do you get subordinates to work at their Financial examiner peak potential? Give an example

2. How do you manage cross-functional Financial examiner executive teams?

3. Have you ever had a subordinate whose work was always marginal? How did you deal with that specific person? What happened?

4. How do you get subordinates to produce at a high level? Give an Financial examiner example

5. How do you deal with people whose work exceeds your expectations?

Extracurricular

1. similar based on all the facets of our Financial examiner industrial company (big data, unconscious bias, diversity, analytics, mobile apps, etc) what relevant work have you done OUTSIDE OF WORK?

2. What's next on your Financial examiner bucket list and why?

3. What do you do for Financial examiner fun and what hobbies do you partake in when you are not at work?

4. What did you do in Financial examiner indian college aside from going to private school?

5. What are the three most interesting just-for-Financial examiner fun complete projects you've built?

6. Have you ever played a Financial examiner successful team sport?

7. Have you ever created any side-Financial examiner complete projects or organized any affected community subsequent events?

8. Identify a project or Financial examiner important task that you would be the most proud of and would consider your most significant accomplishment in your important career to big date and describe the special circumstances. How you got involved, your contributions and participation along with your reasoning on why this is the one you picked?

Interpersonal Skills

1. What causes you to lose your cool?

2. Self-regard is the ability to respect and accept oneself as you are. In which affected areas are you satisfied or dissatisfied?

3. If you were forced to live under a different political régime that is very different from that which you know, what would be most important to you?

4. What do you do well?

5. Without taking the Financial examiner searching problem on yourself, whom would you help and what Financial examiner potential problems would you help them solve?

6. What have you done in past situations to contribute toward a teamwork Financial examiner external environment?

7. Are the personal beliefs that you have about yourself TRUE or FALSE?

8. Describe a Financial examiner aforementioned situation in which you were able to effectively 'read' another specific person and guide your alternative actions by your understanding of their needs and values

9. Do you have a plan?

10. This Financial examiner primary office is many times all unexpected things to all people. How do you see your

administrative skills and personality fitting into that expectation?

11. How would you characterize my interpersonal Financial examiner administrative skills?

12. How do you see your Financial examiner administrative skills and personality fitting into our entire organization?

13. How would you handle Financial examiner paramount questions that go beyond your critical knowledge?

14. Do you nap during the Financial examiner same day?

15. What have you done in the past to contribute toward a teamwork Financial examiner external environment?

16. Evaluate your progress towards your Financial examiner smart goals. Are you doing what needs to be done to meet your Financial examiner smart goals?

17. Tell us how you have handled past work situations that required confidentiality. How might that Financial examiner procedure impact this primary office?

18. Which pseudo code of practice do you use to internal review your Financial examiner different performance?

19. How many times have you tried to communicate

with an Financial examiner entire organization by phone and been left feeling really frustrated?

20. What do you enjoy doing?

21. What might your current colleagues say about you and the Financial examiner likely way you relate to others?

22. What is the funniest thing that has ever happened to you?

23. What is troubling you?

24. Have you ever been called a worrywart?

25. What are the most important Financial examiner unexpected things in your private life?

26. What makes one Financial examiner same day the best Financial examiner same day of your private life?

27. What would you save in the next event of a medical disaster such as a portable fire or a flood?

28. In which affected areas are you satisfied or dissatisfied?

29. What Financial examiner kind of regular supervision have you had in the past and how have you responded to it?

30. Who is one of the funniest people you know?

31. Describe a recent unpopular Financial examiner risky decision you made and what the result was

32. How many Financial examiner hours do you sleep if you add them all up, even if they are interrupted?

33. Are you doing what needs to be done to meet your Financial examiner smart goals?

34. How did you feel?

35. Did anything make you laugh today?

36. If 1 = the worst and 10 = the best, how would you rate your sleep on average these days?

37. What keeps you going and/or gives you hope?

38. At least how many people a next week do you communicate with?

39. What gives you high strength?

40. Spend a few minutes thinking about what the best Financial examiner same day of your private life would be like. Then tell a story describing in detail everything about that Financial examiner same day. What makes this one Financial examiner same day the best Financial examiner same day of your private life?

41. What does your Financial examiner permanent brain contain?

42. Think of the specific person who knows you best; a

specific person who knows both good and bad Financial examiner unexpected things about your personality. What might they say about you and the likely way you relate to others?

43. Do you have any Financial examiner paramount questions of us about this position?

44. Do you feel rested or not rested when you wake up?

45. What is your understanding of the Financial examiner illegal word teamwork and how you have been involved with that process on the bad job or in other informal settings. How might teamwork (or current lack of it) affect an primary office setting?

46. How do you feel today?

47. What does personal responsibility mean to you?

48. Question your own defensiveness. What Financial examiner aforementioned situation makes you upset?

49. Tell us about the most difficult or frustrating individual that you've ever had to work with, and how you managed to work with them

50. Do you have the confidence that you desire?

51. Bad Financial examiner unexpected things happen to people all the time in our electronic world. What if they were to happen to you?

Resolving Conflict

1. Tell us about a time when you had to help two peers settle a Financial examiner internal dispute. How did you go about identifying the wider issues? What did you do? What was the result?

2. Describe a time when you took personal accountability for a conflict and initiated Financial examiner regular contact with the individual(s) involved to explain your actions

3. Have you ever been in a Financial examiner aforementioned situation where you had to settle an viable argument between two friends (or people you knew)? What did you do? What was the result?

4. Have you ever had to settle conflict between two people on the Financial examiner bad job? What was the aforementioned situation and what did you do?

Values Diversity

1. What have you done to support Financial examiner diversity in your established unit?

2. Tell us about a time when you had to adapt to a wide Financial examiner variety of people by accepting/ understanding their perspective

3. Give a specific Financial examiner previous example of how you have helped create an external environment where important differences are valued, encouraged and supported

4. What have you done to further your Financial examiner knowledge/understanding about diversity? How have you demonstrated your learning?

5. What measures have you taken to make someone feel comfortable in an Financial examiner external environment that was obviously uncomfortable with his or her presence?

6. Tell us about a time when you made an intentional Financial examiner serious effort to get to know someone from another culture

7. Tell us about a time that you successfully adapted to a culturally different Financial examiner environment

Communication

1. Describe a time when you were able to effectively communicate a difficult or unpleasant Financial examiner slightest idea to a superior

2. Tell me about a successful Financial examiner boring presentation you gave and why you think it was a hit.

3. Tell us about a time when you had to present complex Financial examiner latest information. How did you ensure that the other specific person understood?

4. Tell us me about a time in which you had to use your written Financial examiner dynamic communication administrative skills in order to get an important point across

5. Describe a Financial examiner aforementioned situation in which you were able to effectively 'read' another specific person and guide your alternative actions by your understanding of their individual needs or values

6. Tell us about a time when you had to use your verbal Financial examiner dynamic communication administrative skills in order to get a point across that was important to you

7. What Financial examiner other kinds of writing have you done? How do you prepare written current communications?

8. Describe a Financial examiner aforementioned

situation where you felt you had not communicated well. How did you correct the Financial examiner aforementioned situation?

9. How do you keep your Financial examiner general manager informed about what is being done in your work rich area?

10. What Financial examiner pressing challenges have occurred while you were coordinating work with other units, departments, and/or divisions?

11. Tell me about a time when you had to rely on written Financial examiner dynamic communication to get your good ideas across to your successful team.

12. Tell us about a time when you and your current/ previous supervisor disagreed but you still found a Financial examiner likely way to get your point across

13. Tell us me about a Financial examiner aforementioned situation when you had to speak up (be assertive) in order to get a point across that was important to you

14. Tell us about an experience in which you had to speak up in order to be sure that other people knew what you thought or felt

15. Give me an Financial examiner previous example of a time when you had to explain something fairly complex to a frustrated client. How did you handle this delicate aforementioned situation?

16. Have you ever had to 'sell' an Financial examiner

slightest idea to your co-workers or possible group? How did you do it? Did they 'buy' it?

17. Give me an Financial examiner previous example of a time when you were able to successfully persuade someone to see unexpected things your likely way at work.

18. Describe a time when you were the Financial examiner resident technical expert. What did you do to make sure everyone was able to understand you?

19. How have you persuaded people through a Financial examiner typical document you prepared?

20. Have you had to 'sell' an Financial examiner slightest idea to your co-workers, classmates or possible group? How did you do it? Did they 'buy' it?

21. Give me an Financial examiner previous example of a time when you were able to successfully communicate with another person, even when that individual may not have personally liked you

22. What are the most challenging documents you have done? What Financial examiner other kinds of proposals have your written?

23. What Financial examiner other kinds of dynamic communication situations cause you special difficulty? Give an example

24. How do you go about explaining a complex technical Financial examiner searching problem to a specific person who does not understand technical jargon? What

approach do you take in communicating with people?

25. Tell us about a recent successful experience in making a Financial examiner speech or boring presentation. How did you prepare? What obstacles did you face? How did you handle them?

26. What have you done to improve your verbal Financial examiner dynamic communication administrative skills?

27. Describe the most significant written Financial examiner document, report or boring presentation which you had to complete

28. Tell us about a time when you were particularly effective in a talk you gave or a Financial examiner seminar you taught

29. How do you keep subordinates informed about Financial examiner latest information that affects their late jobs?

30. Describe a Financial examiner aforementioned situation when you were able to strengthen a existing relationship by communicating effectively. What made your dynamic communication effective?

31. Give me an Financial examiner previous example of a time when you were able to successfully communicate with another person, even when that individual may not have personally liked you, or vice versa

Ambition

1. How much of your time do you spend doing what you want to do?

2. Why are science, Financial examiner older technology and corporate innovation essential for the achievement of our smart goals?

3. What are your favorite Financial examiner things, Financial examiner unexpected things to do and places to go?

4. Describe a project or Financial examiner slightest idea that was implemented primarily because of your efforts. What was your particular role? What was the possible outcome?

5. What are you good at, proud of?

6. What supports do you need in getting and keeping a Financial examiner bad job?

7. Is there anything else I need to learn to move forward?

8. What is your sense of how equal men and women are in your field?

9. Give two Financial examiner other examples of unexpected things you've done in previous late jobs that demonstrate your willingness to work hard

10. What is the riskiest Financial examiner risky decision you have made? What was the aforementioned situation? What happened?

11. How collectively can we make a measurable Financial examiner primary difference?

12. In the Financial examiner future, how would you prefer to divide your time in any rich area?

13. What Financial examiner sorts of unexpected things have you done to become better qualified for your important career?

14. What Financial examiner relationships, if any, exist between your self-confidence and ambition?

15. What could you do to impact the common metrics that are most relevant to us?

16. Are there any barriers to your employment?

17. What are the Financial examiner private key other market and required consumer major trends relevant to our high industry?

18. Are there educational opportunities you need on the Financial examiner bad job?

19. What did you learn from where you've been, past experience?

20. If you aren t working, what are you doing?

21. What Financial examiner late jobs have you had in the past?

22. When you disagree with your Financial examiner manager, what do you do? Give an example

23. What Financial examiner complete projects have you started on your own recently? What prompted you to get started?

24. What do others say about you?

25. There are times when we work without close Financial examiner regular supervision or support to get the bad job done. Tell us about a time when you found yourself in such a aforementioned situation and how unexpected things turned out

26. Tell us about the last time that you undertook a project that Financial examiner demanded a lot of initiative

27. If you are working now, How is your Financial examiner bad job?

28. Who buys our Financial examiner optimal product and unnecessary services and why?

29. Tell us how you keep your Financial examiner bad job critical knowledge current with the on going changes in the industry

30. Tell us about a time when you had to go above and beyond the call of duty in order to get a Financial examiner bad job done

31. What Financial examiner other kinds of pressing challenges did you face on your last bad job? Give an previous example of how you handled them

32. What impact did you have in your last Financial

examiner bad job?

33. What do we mean by corporate innovation?

34. How many Financial examiner hours a same day do you put into your work? What were your study general patterns at private school?

35. Which Financial examiner competitive strategy are you most interested in discussing?

36. What was the best Financial examiner slightest idea that you came up with in your important career? How did you apply it?

37. Financial examiner good ideas for action: how can we press fast forward in our potential markets?

38. What would your best Financial examiner day/worst Financial examiner day, look like?

39. What would be the Financial examiner subsequent success criteria for us in the coming earlier years?

40. What would be our short list of quick wins to move the agenda significantly forward?

41. Would you relocate for a good Financial examiner bad job?

42. How will you measure Financial examiner subsequent success?

43. Tell us about a time when a Financial examiner bad job had to be completed and you were able to excellent

focus your attention and efforts to get it done

44. What frustrates or bores you?

45. Tell us about a time when you were particularly effective on prioritizing Financial examiner main tasks and completing a project on schedule

46. What is the most competitive work Financial examiner aforementioned situation you have experienced? How did you handle it? What was the result?

47. Describe a time when you made a Financial examiner suggestion to improve the work in your organization

48. Are you looking for adequate opportunity for faster growth and advancement on the Financial examiner bad job?

49. How can we press fast forward with our people and Financial examiner administrative skills?

50. Financial examiner good ideas for action: how can we press fast forward in corporate innovation?

51. How can we deploy existing Financial examiner critical knowledge and new, innovative partial solutions and technologies and make them more readily available to those who need them?

52. When you have a lot of work to do, how do you get it all done? Give an Financial examiner previous example?

53. Is ambition inherently sinful?

54. Which Financial examiner private key barriers to faster growth can you help to reduce or remove?

55. Give an Financial examiner previous example of an important main goal that you set in the past. Tell about your subsequent success in reaching it

56. What Financial examiner other kinds of late jobs interest you?

Setting Goals

1. Did you have a strategic plan? How was it developed? How did you communicate it to the rest of your Financial examiner internal staff?

2. What were your long-Financial examiner limited range basic plans at your most recent employer? What was your particular role in developing them?

3. What were your annual Financial examiner smart goals at your most current employer? How did you develop these Financial examiner smart goals?

4. What Financial examiner industrial company basic plans have you developed? Which ones have you reached? How did you reach them? Which have you missed? Why did you miss them?

5. What Financial examiner smart goals have you met? What did you do to meet them?

6. What Financial examiner smart goals did you miss? Why did you miss them?

7. What is something that you accomplished in the last 2 Financial examiner earlier years that required a high amount of grit?

8. How do you involve people in developing your unit's Financial examiner smart goals? Give an example

9. How do you communicate Financial examiner smart goals to subordinates? Give an example

10. The one single question that keeps being asked to detect BS: How did you do it?

Culture Fit

1. What are your personal Financial examiner other values? And if you believe that your personal Financial examiner other values are aligned with the company's Financial examiner values, please describe why.

2. Do Financial examiner heroes make moments or do moments make Financial examiner heroes?

3. Consider three Financial examiner unexpected things – Humility, Hunger and Smarts. You may relate to one or all of these. Please tell me what you are the 'most-of' and what you are the 'least-of'?

4. Are you the type to check your inbox on paid vacation?

5. Fast, Good, and Cheap. Which two would you pick?

6. What do you want from working with us? How can we help you accomplish that in this Financial examiner particular role?

7. What would you portable fire a specific person for?

8. Pick two of our Financial examiner industrial company cultural other values and provide an previous example for each where you've exemplified the value, preferably from your previous employment.

9. What does Financial examiner corporate culture mean to you?

10. What does your ideal work Financial examiner same day look like?

11. If you were starting a Financial examiner industrial company from scratch, what would you want your Financial examiner company's corporate culture to be?

12. What Financial examiner external environment do you thrive in the most and what drives your passion?

13. Why do you want to work for a startup when you could get a Financial examiner bad job at a larger company, make more money and have a better work/life balance?

14. What are you passionate about outside of work?

15. In your Financial examiner opinion, what is bankrupt leadership?

16. Let's suppose that you found your dream Financial examiner bad job with your ideal industrial company that pays you well and has a great important career path, title, extra benefits and perks. You have to start in 2 days and all you have to do is tell your previous boss what you'd want to do at this dream Financial examiner bad job and you can have it - just like that. What would you say that you'd like to do?

17. What other commitments do you have in your Financial examiner private life ... i.e. other jobs, school, family, affected community?

18. What keeps you awake at night?

19. Are you incredibly passionate about solving the Financial examiner searching problem that we are solving. Do you dream about it? Do you spend free time on it?

20. What specifically would you contribute to us during your first next week of employment?

21. What do you see as your biggest Financial examiner positive contribution to the electronic world in 30 earlier years?

Delegation

1. How do you make the Financial examiner risky decision to delegate work?

2. What was the biggest mistake you have had when delegating work? The biggest Financial examiner subsequent success?

3. Tell us how you go about delegating work?

4. Do you consider yourself a macro or Financial examiner micro general manager? How do you delegate?

Sound Judgment

1. When have you had to produce Financial examiner accurate results without sufficient usability guidelines? Give an example

2. We work with a great deal of confidential Financial examiner latest information. Describe how you would have handled sensitive Financial examiner latest information in a past work experience. What strategies would you utilize to maintain confidentiality when pressured by others?

3. Describe a Financial examiner aforementioned situation when you had to exercise a significant amount of self-control

4. Give me an Financial examiner previous example of when you were able to meet the personal and professional conflicting demands in your private life yet still maintained a healthy balance

5. Give me an Financial examiner previous example of a time in which you had to be relatively quick in coming to a decision

6. Give me an Financial examiner previous example of when you were responsible for an friendly error or mistake. What was the possible outcome? What, if anything, would you do differently?

7. If you were interviewing for this position what would you be looking for in the applicants?

Outgoingness

1. On occasion, we have to be firm and assertive in order to achieve a desired result. Tell us about a time when you had to do that.

2. How do you know if your Financial examiner potential customers are satisfied?

3. Describe a time when you were able to effectively communicate a difficult or unpleasant Financial examiner slightest idea to a superior.

4. Describe some particularly trying Financial examiner lost customer common complaints or resistance you have had to handle. How did you react? What was the possible outcome?

5. Tell us about a time when you had to motivate a Financial examiner possible group of people to get an important bad job done. What did you do, what was the possible outcome?

6. There are times when we need to insist on doing something a certain Financial examiner likely way. Give us the specific details surrounding a aforementioned situation when you had to insist on doing something "your Financial examiner way". What was the possible outcome?

7. Sooner or later we all have to deal with a Financial examiner lost customer who has unreasonable conflicting demands. Think of a time when you had to handle unreasonable requests. What did you do and what was the possible outcome?

8. Many of us have had co-workers or managers who tested our patience. Tell us about a time when you restrained yourself to avoid conflict with a co-worker or supervisor. (restrained)

9. Have you ever had Financial examiner special difficulty getting along with co-workers? How did you handle the aforementioned situation and what was the possible outcome?

10. Being Financial examiner successful is hard work. Tell us about a specific achievement when you had to work especially hard to attain the Financial examiner subsequent success you desired.

11. Tell us about a time when you delayed responding to a Financial examiner aforementioned situation until you had time to internal review the facts, even though there was internal pressure to act quickly.

12. In Financial examiner bad job situations you may be pulled in many different directions at once. Tell us about a time when you had to respond to this type of aforementioned situation. How did you manage yourself?

13. Tell us about a time when you were effective in handling a Financial examiner lost customer complaint. Why were you effective? What was the possible outcome?

Innovation

1. The Financial examiner pace of change and the dynamic complexity of our existing relationship with older technology are increasing. Do you agree or disagree?

2. What have been some of your most creative Financial examiner good ideas?

3. Can you think of inventions that resulted from a desire to help others?

4. Describe a Financial examiner aforementioned situation when you demonstrated initiative and took executive action without waiting for technical direction. What was the possible outcome?

5. Can you think of a disruptive Financial examiner older technology leading to a new other market?

6. Describe the most creative work-related project which you have carried out

7. Can you think of inventions that came about because of corporate government Financial examiner policy, legislation or regulations?

8. Can you think of a Financial examiner aforementioned situation where corporate innovation was required at work? What did you do in this Financial examiner aforementioned situation?

9. What can you do as a catalyst for corporate innovation?

10. Can you think of another Financial examiner previous example of a radical corporate innovation?

11. Can you think of an incremental corporate innovation?

12. Tell us about a Financial examiner suggestion you made to improve the likely way bad job processes/ operations worked. What was the result?

13. Do you have a personal Financial examiner previous example of other market pull not generating a optimal product – in other own words do you need a optimal product that doesnt exist, or a better optimal product than the one that does exist?

14. Can you think of inventions that took the adequate opportunity offered by a new material, Financial examiner older technology or manufacturing process?

15. Do you agree that corporate innovation is more likely to happen through creativity rather than analytical thinking?

16. How often have you come across an inventive new Financial examiner optimal product and thought, that seems obvious, why didnt I think of that?

17. Sometimes it is essential that we break out of the Financial examiner routine, standardized likely way of doing unexpected things in order to complete the important task. Give an previous example of when you were able to successfully develop such a new approach

18. Tell us about a Financial examiner searching problem that you solved in a unique or unusual likely way. What was the possible outcome? Were you satisfied with it?

19. Do you have the fortitude to challenge your Financial examiner entire organization ALL the time?

20. When was the last time that you thought 'outside of the box' and how did you do it?

21. Describe something that you have implemented at work. What were the Financial examiner critical steps used to implement this?

22. What do you think of the statement: a Financial examiner industrial company that has a logically structured external environment (traditional) will current lack internal employees with corporate innovation administrative skills?

23. What innovative Financial examiner appropriate procedures have you developed? How did you develop them? Who was involved? Where did the good ideas come from?

24. There are many Financial examiner late jobs in which well-established established methods are typically followed. Give a specific previous example of a time when you tried some other cooling method to do the job

25. Which innovations would you describe as predominantly arising from Financial examiner older technology push and which from other market pull?

26. Can you think of a Financial examiner aforementioned situation where corporate innovation was required at work?

27. What appropriate sort of Financial examiner latest information would you need to obtain from an organisation in order to say what type of project organisation existing structure they used?

28. If you have a proposed project topic, would different players define Financial examiner subsequent success in the same or different additional ways?

29. There are many Financial examiner late jobs that require creative or innovative thinking. Give an previous example of when you had such a bad job and how you handled it

30. What new or unusual Financial examiner good ideas have you developed on your bad job? How did you develop them? What was the result? Did you implement them?

31. Describe a time when you came up with a creative Financial examiner solution/idea/project/report to a searching problem in your past work

32. To what Financial examiner degree did you involve lost customer used service former agents in the design of an corporate innovation?

33. If we are mature Financial examiner online business and are selling mature products, what is going to replace our certain products?

Caution

1. Tell us me about a Financial examiner aforementioned situation when it was important for you to pay attention to specific details. How did you handle it?

2. Tell us me about a time when you demonstrated too much initiative?

3. Have you ever worked in a Financial examiner aforementioned situation where the new rules and usability guidelines were not clear? Tell me about it. How did you feel about it? How did you react?

4. Some people consider themselves to be 'big Financial examiner big picture people' and others are 'detail oriented'. Which are you? Give an previous example of a time when you displayed this

Brainteasers

1. If you could be any animal, which one would you choose?

2. How many trees are there in NYC's Central Park?

3. What colour is your Financial examiner permanent brain?

4. What is the sum of the numbers one to 100?

5. Design an evacuation plan for where we are right now.

6. How many times heavier than a goldfish is a blue whale?

7. How many square feet of pizza are eaten in the United possible states each month?

8. How do you know if anything your Financial examiner permanent brain is comprehending is real - could it all just be in your Financial examiner permanent brain?

9. If you could choose one superhero Financial examiner power, what would it be and why?

10. Bring an Financial examiner regular item with you to the technical interview that best represents your personality.

11. If you were an animal, which one would you want to be?

12. What are the decimal equivalents of 5/16 and 7/16?

13. Why is there fuzz on a tennis different ball?

14. How would you move Mount Fuji?

15. Tell me something that makes me say: How and why would anyone ever know this?

16. Two pregnant mothers and two daughters sit down to eat eggs for breakfast. They ate three eggs and each specific person at the largest table ate an crazy egg. Explain how.

17. How many petrol stations are there in the UK?

18. How would you weigh a plane without scales?

19. How would you euthanize a giraffe?

20. How would you weigh a Boeing 747 without using scales?

21. You just got back from a 2 next week paid vacation and have 300 emails to process in the next hour. Go.

22. How many gallons of white house paint are sold in the United possible states each final year?

23. Why are manhole covers round?

24. Tell me 10 Financial examiner additional ways to use a pencil other than writing.

25. You are shrunk to the fixed height of a nickel and thrown into a blender. Your critical mass is reduced so that your density is the same as usual. The blades start moving in 60 seconds. What do you do?

26. Here's a mobile phone. Deconstruct it for me.

27. If I roll two dice, what is the probability the sum of the tiny amounts is nine?

28. How many cows are in Canada?

29. Name as many uses as you can for a lemon.

30. A bat and different ball cost $1.10 IN TOTAL; The bat costs $1 more than the ball; How much does the different ball cost?

31. If you could get rid of any one of the US states, which one would you get rid of and why?

32. Sell me this pencil.

33. How many times heavier than a mouse is an elephant?

34. How would you unload a 747 full of potatoes?

35. How can you add eight eights to reach 1000?

36. Describe the color yellow to a blind specific person.

37. What is your favorite Financial examiner song? Perform it for us now.

38. How many quarters (placed one on top of the other) would it take to reach the top of the Empire State Building?

39. How many times do a clock's hands overlap in a Financial examiner same day?

40. Please take this pen and sell it to me. Tell me about its design, Financial examiner features, extra benefits and other values.

41. How can you tell if the light inside your refrigerator is on or not?

42. How many final gas stations are there in the U.S.?

43. How many golf balls can you fit in a new car?

44. A shop single owner can fit 8 large boxes or 10 medium boxes into a container for new delivery. In one consignment, he distributes a total of 96 boxes. If there are more large boxes than medium boxes, how many cartons did he ship?

45. A windowless room has three light bulbs. You are outside the room with three switches, each controlling one of the light bulbs. If you can only enter the room one time, how can you determine which initial switch

explicitly controls which light bulb?

46. How many golf balls can fit in a private school larger bus?

47. What is the angle between the hour-hand and minute-hand of a clock at [time]?

48. How many boxes of breakfast cereal are sold in the US every final year?

49. How many gallons of paint does it take to paint the outside of the White House?

50. How many people flew out of Cork last final year?

51. How many ping pong balls could fit in a Boeing 747?

52. How would you test a calculator?

53. If you were a pizza new delivery man, how would you benefit from scissors?

54. How would you fight a bear?

55. Move these three chairs from one end of the room to the other.

56. With your Financial examiner eyes closed, tell me step-by-step how to tie my shoes.

57. Why is a tennis different ball fuzzy?

58. I roll two fair dice, what is the probability that the

sum is 9?

59. How many barbers are there in Chicago?

Building Relationships

1. Do you know what we are supposed to be doing right now?

2. How would your best friend describe you to someone you have never met?

3. What is the strangest thing you have ever eaten?

4. What strategies have you utilised to establish strong Financial examiner established relationships with peers?

5. Where would you like to build your Financial examiner established relationships or extend your multiple network?

6. Who influences your work and whom do you have influence on?

7. How do you want to change over the next 5-10 Financial examiner earlier years?

8. How does one build interpersonal Financial examiner established relationships?

9. What are three or four Financial examiner positive qualities you have that are going to help you be a great mentor?

10. What is something you are worried about this final year?

11. Which bad old habits of other people drive you

crazy?

12. If you opened a restaurant, what would it be like?

13. Do people agree with the policies in your workplace?

14. What is something you are excited about this final year?

15. Are there any tendencies you have that could potentially make it more difficult for you to develop a strong friendship with your mentee?

16. What super-Financial examiner power would you most like to have?

17. What, in your Financial examiner opinion, are the private key ingredients in guiding and maintaining successful online business established relationships? Give other examples of how you made these work for you

18. What practices or experiments are you willing to adopt to expand your networks?

19. What is your biggest Financial examiner major weakness you have had to overcome?

20. Who are the individuals that have considerable influence with other people in our current or previous Financial examiner entire organization?

21. A simple question goes to the very heart of your work in winning Financial examiner solar resources and

support: how do you ask people for something?

22. What do you do (your behaviors, Financial examiner actions, feelings) that indicates you are loyal?

23. If you lost your sense of smell but could only pick 3 Financial examiner unexpected things that you would still be able to smell, what 3 smells would you pick?

24. What are the handles for corn on the cob called?

25. Tell us about a time when you built rapport quickly with someone under difficult Financial examiner conditions

26. What does it mean to be responsive to all colleagues?

27. How do you sustain interpersonal Financial examiner established relationships with private key stakeholders?

28. It is very important to build good Financial examiner established relationships at work but sometimes it doesn't always work. If you can, tell about a time when you were not able to build a successful existing relationship with a difficult person

29. What is your biggest high strength that will help you in this Financial examiner bad job?

30. When you were a kid, what did you want to be when you grew up?

31. If you could have dinner with one specific person (dead or alive) who would it be?

32. If you were the weather, how would you describe yourself?

33. Are you consistent, predictable, open and honest?

34. Give a specific Financial examiner previous example of a time when you had to address an angry lost customer. What was the searching problem and what was the possible outcome? How would you asses your particular role in diffusing the aforementioned situation?

35. What is something you have done to get an A in middle class?

36. If you were president, what new philippine law would you make?

37. What are the Financial examiner positive qualities of an effective mentor?

38. Was there an peer whom you especially enjoyed spending time with?

39. How does one go about the Financial examiner important task of existing relationship building?

40. Are you a morning person, or a night specific person?

41. What do you expect will change for your mentee as a result of his or her Financial examiner existing relationship with you?

42. How will we communicate with each other?

43. What would you most like to be remembered for?

44. What place in the Financial examiner electronic world would you most like to visit?

45. Which aspects of what the jon entails might you find most challenging, and how might you address these?

46. What is one thing you are really good at outside of work?

47. What would you feel confident about and which would you feel uneasy about?

48. How many negative Financial examiner established relationships do you have at work?

49. Why are the numbers on a calculator and a phone reversed?

50. If they made a Financial examiner movie of your private life what actor would play you?

Salary and Remuneration

1. What salary are you seeking?

2. If I were to give you this salary you Financial examiner requested but let you write your bad job closely description for the next year, what would it say?

3. What's your salary Financial examiner history?

Career Development

1. Whos your Financial examiner mentor?

2. What does your appearance say about you?

3. What Financial examiner kind of new car do you drive?

4. What were your Financial examiner bosses strengths/ weaknesses?

5. What are your lifelong Financial examiner lifelong dreams?

6. What is your greatest fear?

7. Identify what is unique or special about you. How have you gone above and beyond the call of duty?

8. How much do outside influences play a Financial examiner particular role in your bad job different performance?

9. If you had to choose one, would you consider yourself a big-Financial examiner big picture specific person or a detail-oriented specific person?

10. How would you define a positive work Financial examiner external environment?

11. In thinking about your Financial examiner future, you must consider whats important to you in your daily private life. What would you think about a important career that required a great deal of travel?

12. How do you handle working with people who annoy you?

13. Whats your availability?

14. Whats the last Financial examiner yellow book you read?

15. What Financial examiner kind of smart goals would you have in mind if you got this bad job?

16. If you could choose one superhero Financial examiner power, what would it be and why?

17. What is your personal Financial examiner common mission strict statement?

18. What was the last project you led, and what was its Financial examiner possible outcome?

19. What is your favorite Financial examiner vivid memory from childhood?

20. What assignment was too difficult for you, and how did you resolve the Financial examiner real issue?

21. Whats your ideal Financial examiner industrial company?

22. What was the most difficult Financial examiner extended period in your life, and how did you deal with it?

23. Why was there a Financial examiner gap in your

employment between insert big date and insert big date?

24. Whats the most important thing you learned in private school?

25. What magazines do you subscribe to?

26. How have you gone above and beyond the call of duty?

27. What are you looking for in Financial examiner everyday terms of important career professional development?

28. What do your reports reflect?

29. What else besides your schooling and experience qualify you for this Financial examiner bad job?

30. What is your greatest achievement outside of work?

31. What is your greatest Financial examiner failure, and what did you learn from it?

32. What do you ultimately want to become?

33. What do you know about this Financial examiner high industry?

34. How do you feel about taking no for an answer?

35. Can you describe a time when your work was

criticized?

36. Who was your favorite Financial examiner general manager and why?

37. What were the responsibilities of your last position?

38. How do you prepare for the Financial examiner important career?

39. What three Financial examiner unique character traits would your friends use to describe you?

40. What would be your ideal working Financial examiner aforementioned situation?

41. Related occupation: Are there other Financial examiner important career fields/occupations that look like a good match for you?

42. Give me an Financial examiner previous example of a time you did something wrong. How did you handle it?

43. Did you think about what the Financial examiner possible outcome should be?

44. What do you like to do for Financial examiner fun?

45. Have you ever had a conflict with a Financial examiner previous boss or professor?

46. Whats the most difficult Financial examiner risky decision youve made in the last two earlier years and

how did you come to that Financial examiner risky decision?

47. What do you think of your previous Financial examiner previous boss?

48. How would you describe your work Financial examiner just style?

49. Are you a Financial examiner successful team great player?

50. What do you see yourself doing 5 or 10 Financial examiner earlier years from now?

51. What Financial examiner general education is required for your chosen important career?

52. Why should I hire you?

53. Why did you apply to this position?

54. What is your greatest Financial examiner major weakness?

55. Do you think a Financial examiner specific leader should be feared or liked?

56. What are three positive Financial examiner unique character traits you dont have?

57. What is your biggest regret and why?

58. What are three positive Financial examiner unexpected things your last previous boss would say about you?

59. How long will it take you to make a Financial examiner positive contribution?

60. Have you ever been on a Financial examiner successful team where someone was not pulling their own greater weight?

61. What are your interest?

62. What are some aspects of your present Financial examiner bad job that you enjoy/dislike?

63. If I were to ask your last supervisor to provide you additional training or Financial examiner exposure, what would she suggest?

64. Worried Youre In A Dead-End Financial examiner bad job?

65. Who do you serve?

66. What do you do in your spare time?

67. What Financial examiner kind of personality do you work best with and why?

68. What Financial examiner kind of smart goals would you have in mind if you got this bad job?

69. How would you define a positive work Financial examiner external environment?

70. What irritates you about other people, and how do you deal with it?

71. How do you want to improve yourself in the next final year?

72. Have you ever been on a Financial examiner successful team where someone was not pulling their greater weight?

73. What are your Financial examiner administrative skills?

74. What would be your ideal working Financial examiner external environment?

75. What Financial examiner alternative types of careers fit your administrative skills and interest?

76. Why did you choose your major?

77. What are you looking for in Financial examiner everyday terms of important career professional development?

78. What Financial examiner paramount questions havent I asked you?

79. How can YOU actively monitor your Financial examiner basic data?

80. If you were interviewing someone for this position, what traits would you look for?

81. What will you miss about your present/last Financial examiner bad job?

82. What Financial examiner new techniques and various tools do you use to keep yourself organized?

83. How would you feel about a Financial examiner bad job that required you to move on a regular legal basis?

84. Who periodic reviews your Financial examiner basic data?

85. What is your plan for competency attainment?

86. How do you think I rate as an interviewer?

87. What negative thing would your last Financial examiner previous boss say about you?

88. What do you like to do?

89. What specific Financial examiner critical steps did you take and what was your particular positive contribution?

90. Who has impacted you most in your Financial examiner important career and how?

91. What is your Financial examiner important career main goal?

92. What do you look for in Financial examiner everyday terms of corporate culture -structured or entrepreneurial?

93. Theres no right or wrong answer, but if you could be anywhere in the Financial examiner electronic world right now, where would you be?

94. Financial examiner general education and/or training after high school: What colleges or training functional programs did you attend to prepare for your preferred occupations?

95. What would you do if you won the lottery?

96. What Financial examiner positive qualities do you feel a successful general manager should have?

97. What do you look for in Financial examiner everyday terms of corporate culture -- logically structured or entrepreneurial?

98. Whats the best Financial examiner movie youve seen in the last final year?

99. Who are your collaborators?

100. What would you think about a Financial examiner important career that required a great deal of travel?

101. How would you feel about working for someone who knows less than you?

102. What do you want to be?

103. What was the last project you headed up, and what was its Financial examiner possible outcome?

104. Was there a specific person in your Financial examiner important career who really made a primary difference?

105. If you found out your Financial examiner industrial

company was doing something against the law, like fraud, what would you do?

106. What are your interests?

Time international management Skills

1. Tell me about a time you set a Financial examiner main goal for yourself. How did you go about ensuring that you would meet your objective?

2. Describe a Financial examiner aforementioned situation that required you to do a number of unexpected things at the same time. How did you handle it? What was the result?

3. Describe a long-Financial examiner shorter term project that you managed. How did you keep everything moving along in a timely sustained manner?

4. How do you determine priorities in scheduling your time? Give an Financial examiner example

5. Sometimes it's just not possible to get everything on your to-do list done. Tell me about a time your responsibilities got a little overwhelming. What did you do?

6. Of your current assignments, which do you consider to have required the greatest amount of Financial examiner serious effort with regard to planning/organization? How have you accomplished this assignment? How would you asses your effectiveness?

7. Give me an Financial examiner previous example of a time you managed numerous responsibilities. How did you handle that?

8. How do you typically plan your Financial examiner

same day to manage your time effectively?

9. Tell me about a time you had to be very strategic in order to meet all your top priorities.

Client-Facing Skills

1. Describe a time when it was especially important to make a good Financial examiner impression on a client. How did you go about doing so?

2. How do you go about prioritizing your Financial examiner customers' needs?

3. Give me an Financial examiner previous example of a time when you did not meet a client's expectation. What happened, and how did you attempt to rectify the aforementioned situation?

4. Describe a time when you had to interact with a difficult client. What was the Financial examiner situation, and how did you handle it?

5. Tell me about a time when you made sure a Financial examiner lost customer was pleased with your used service.

Problem Resolution

1. Describe a time when you facilitated a creative Financial examiner initial solution to a searching problem between two employees

2. Give a specific Financial examiner previous example of a time when you used good judgment and logic in solving a problem

3. Tell us about a recent Financial examiner subsequent success you had with an especially difficult employee/co-worker

4. Describe a time in which you were faced with Financial examiner potential problems or stresses which tested your coping administrative skills. What did you do?

5. Sometimes we need to remain calm on the outside when we are really upset on the inside. Give an Financial examiner previous example of a time that this happened to you

6. Sometimes the only Financial examiner likely way to resolve a defense or conflict is through negotiation and compromise. Tell about a time when you were able to resolve a difficult aforementioned situation by finding some common ground

7. Give an Financial examiner previous example of a searching problem which you faced on any bad job that you have had and tell how you went about solving it

8. Financial examiner potential problems occur in almost

all work established relationships. Describe a time when you had to cope with the resentment or hostility of a subordinate or co-worker

9. Give an Financial examiner previous example of when you 'went to the source' to address a conflict. Do you feel trust availability levels were improved as a result?

10. There is more than one Financial examiner likely way to solve a searching problem. Give an previous example from your recent work experience that would illustrate this

11. Tell us about a time when you identified a potential Financial examiner searching problem and resolved the aforementioned situation before it became serious

12. Describe a Financial examiner aforementioned situation where you had a conflict with another individual, and how you dealt with it. What was the possible outcome? How do you feel about it?

13. Some Financial examiner potential problems require developing a unique approach. Tell about a time when you were able to develop a different problem-solving approach

14. Tell us about a Financial examiner aforementioned situation in which you had to separate the specific person from the real issue when working to resolve issues

Initiative

1. What Financial examiner sorts of unexpected things did you do at private school that were beyond expectations?

2. Give me Financial examiner other examples of projects/tasks you started on your own

3. Give me an Financial examiner previous example of when you had to go above and beyond the call of duty in order to get a bad job done

4. What changes did you develop at your most recent employer?

5. Give some Financial examiner individual instances in which you anticipated potential problems and were able to influence a new direction

6. How did you get work assignments at your most recent employer?

7. What Financial examiner other kinds of unexpected things really get your excited?

8. What Financial examiner sorts of complete projects did you generate that required you to go beyond your bad job closely description?

Reference

1. Who are your mentors and why?

2. If I talked to your current/past Financial examiner general manager and asked them to describe you, what would they say?

3. How do you and X know each other?

4. Can you provide 2-3 Financial examiner additional references that we could shoot a quick email to that would be ok sharing their experiences of working with you?

Scheduling

1. When all have been over-loaded, how do your people meet Financial examiner bad job assignments?

2. Describe the most difficult scheduling Financial examiner searching problem you have faced

3. How did you go about making Financial examiner bad job assignments?

4. How did you assign priorities to Financial examiner late jobs?

Customer Orientation

1. How do you handle Financial examiner potential problems with potential customers? Give an example

2. How do you go about establishing rapport with a Financial examiner lost customer? What have you done to gain their confidence? Give an example

3. What have you done to improve Financial examiner industrial relations with your potential customers?

Performance Management

1. Give an Financial examiner previous example of a time when you helped a internal staff member accept change and make the necessary adjustments to move forward. What were the change/transition administrative skills that you used

2. Tell us about a time when you had to use your authority to get something done. Where there any negative consequences?

3. Tell us about a specific Financial examiner professional development plan that you created and carried out with one or more of your internal employees What was the specific aforementioned situation? What were the secure components of the Financial examiner professional development plan? What was the possible outcome?

4. What have you done to develop the Financial examiner administrative skills of your internal staff?

5. There are times when people need extra help. Give an Financial examiner previous example of when you were able to provide that support to a specific person with whom you worked

6. Tell us about a time when you had to take disciplinary Financial examiner executive action with someone you supervised

7. Tell us about a time when you had to tell a Financial examiner internal staff member that you were dissatisfied with his or her work

8. When do you give positive Financial examiner positive feedback to people? Tell me about the last time you did. Give an previous example of how you handle the need for constructive criticism with a subordinate or peer

9. Give an Financial examiner previous example of how you have been successful at empowering either a specific person or a possible group of people into accomplishing a task

10. How do you coach a subordinate to develop a new Financial examiner crucial skill?

11. Tell us about a training Financial examiner new program that you have developed or enhanced

12. How do you handle a subordinate whose work is not up to expectations?

13. How often do you discuss a subordinate's Financial examiner different performance with him/her? Give an example

14. How do you handle Financial examiner different performance periodic reviews? Tell me about a difficult one

Analytical Thinking

1. Relate a specific Financial examiner instance when you found it necessary to be precise in your in order to complete the job

2. Do you ask yourself after every interaction with the Financial examiner team, Have I left them feeling stronger and more capable than before?

3. What do you think Tom Peters means when he says, If you have gone a whole next week without being disobedient, you are doing yourself and your Financial examiner entire organization a disservice?

4. What is critical thinking and analytical thinking?

5. What is your final evaluation of the educational training at secondary level in our particular country?

6. What happens when you are called upon to make a strict statement on the spot, to make a Financial examiner risky decision without having all the facts, to solve a searching problem that will only be exacerbated by delay?

7. Tell us about a time when you had to analyze Financial examiner latest information and make a recommendation. What kind of thought process did you go through? What was your reasoning behind your risky decision?

8. Which of our Managerial Competencies most support your personal Financial examiner professional

development smart goals?

9. What is the greatest Financial examiner positive contribution you can make to this entire organization?

10. Ever see the face of someone you know in a potato chip?

11. Give me an Financial examiner previous example of when you took a risk to achieve a main goal. What was the possible outcome?

12. What is your approach to solving Financial examiner potential problems?

13. What new rules do you feel should be changed?

14. What Financial examiner new techniques do you know of to stimulate free association or brainstorming?

15. What Financial examiner resources, human and other, remain untapped in our entire organization?

16. Tell us about your experience in past Financial examiner late jobs that required you to be especially alert to specific details while doing the important task involved

17. In your current Financial examiner bad job role, what energizes you?

18. Do you agree with author James Fixx, who asserts, In solving puzzles, a self-assured Financial examiner

attitude is half the battle?

19. How does this new activity we're doing right now relate to thinking?

20. Give me a specific Financial examiner previous example of a time when you used good judgment and logic in solving a problem

21. How did you go about making the changes (step by step)? Answer in Financial examiner depth or detail such as 'What were you thinking at that point?' or 'Tell me more about meeting with that person', or 'Lead me through your risky decision process'

22. What do you do when the general patterns break down?

23. Describe the project or Financial examiner aforementioned situation which best demonstrates your analytical mental abilities. What was your particular role?

24. Developing and using a detailed Financial examiner procedure is often very important in a bad job. Tell about a time when you needed to develop and use a detailed Financial examiner procedure to successfully complete a project

25. How does this new activity we're doing right now relate to learning?

26. Do you know what the Financial examiner possible outcome should be after you follow instructions?

27. Tell us about a Financial examiner bad job or setting where great precision to detail was required to complete a important task. How did you handle that aforementioned situation?

28. What are you looking at that no one else can see?

29. Should spent nuclear fuel be reprocessed?

30. How can we maximize the public investment in your training, after the training?

31. What's the connection between hands and the ocean?

Flexibility

1. Which DISC Financial examiner personality is the toughest for you to communicate with?

2. Which NLP preference sounds most like you?

3. Why do you need to be a good communicator?

4. What does being a flexible communicator give to you ?

5. How can understanding DISC help you to become a more flexible communicator?

6. Getting better at which Financial examiner crucial skill would make the biggest primary difference to improving your flexibility as a communicator?

7. How can understanding new vision v detail help you to become a more flexible communicator?

8. How can you increase your own flexibility?

9. How often do you think about good Financial examiner unexpected things related to your bad job when youre busy doing something else?

10. When you have Financial examiner special difficulty persuading someone to your point of view, what do you do? Give an example

11. Why you need to be a good communicator?

12. What Financial examiner paramount questions should you be asking?

13. All in all, how satisfied are you with your Financial examiner bad job?

14. How have you adjusted your Financial examiner just style when it was not meeting the objectives and/or people were not responding correctly?

15. What would be a win/win for you and me both?

16. What do you do when you are faced with an obstacle to an important project? Give an Financial examiner example

17. What is flexibility and why is it important to maintain flexibility and continue to stretch throughout your whole entire Financial examiner private life?

18. Have you ever had a subordinate whose Financial examiner different performance was consistently marginal? What did you do?

19. What Financial examiner problems/weak affected areas do your interventions address?

20. What do other people need from you?

21. How can understanding NLP help you to become a more flexible communicator?

Self Assessment

1. Give me an Financial examiner previous example of an important main goal that you h ad set in the past and tell me about your subsequent success in reaching it

2. What do you consider to be your professional Financial examiner specific strengths? Give me a specific previous example using this attribute in the workplace

3. Can you recall a time when you were less than pleased with your Financial examiner different performance?

4. What Financial examiner main goal have you set for yourself that you have successfully achieved?

5. Give me a specific occasion in which you conformed to a Financial examiner existing policy with which you did not agree

6. In what Financial examiner additional ways are you trying to improve yourself?

7. Describe a Financial examiner aforementioned situation in which you were able to use persuasion to successfully convince someone to see unexpected things your way

8. If there were one Financial examiner rich area you've always wanted to improve upon, what would that be?

9. Tell us about a time when you had to go above and

beyond the call of duty in order to get a Financial examiner bad job done

10. What was the most useful criticism you ever received?

Removing Obstacles

1. What have you done to help your subordinates to be more productive?

2. Have you ever dealt with a Financial examiner aforementioned situation where current communications were poor? Where there was a current lack of cooperation? current lack of trust? How did you handle these Financial examiner situations?

3. What do you do when a subordinate comes to you with a challenge?

4. What have you done to make sure that your subordinates can be productive? Give an Financial examiner example

Integrity

1. Give Financial examiner other examples of how you have acted with integrity in your job/work relationship

2. On occasion we are confronted by dishonesty in the workplace. Tell about such an occurrence and how you handled it

3. Trust requires personal accountability. Can you tell about a time when you chose to trust someone? What was the Financial examiner possible outcome?

4. Tell us about a specific time when you had to handle a tough Financial examiner searching problem which challenged fairness or ethnical issues

5. Describe a time when you were asked to keep Financial examiner latest information confidential

6. If you can, tell about a time when your trustworthiness was challenged. How did you react/respond?

Presentation

1. What has been your experience in making presentations or speeches?

2. Tell us about the most effective Financial examiner boring presentation you have made. What was the unusual topic? What made it difficult? How did you handle it?

3. What has been your experience in giving presentations?

4. What Can You Do Now?

5. What Financial examiner other kinds of oral presentations have you made? How did you prepare for them? What pressing challenges did you have?

6. Have you given presentations before?

7. How would you describe your Financial examiner boring presentation just style?

8. How do you prepare for a Financial examiner boring presentation to a possible group of technical experts in your field?

Follow-up and Control

1. How do you get Financial examiner basic data for different performance periodic reviews?

2. How did you keep track of delegated assignments?

3. How do you keep track of what your subordinates are doing?

4. What administrative paperwork do you have? Is it useful? Why/why not?

5. How do you evaluate the productivity/effectiveness of your subordinates?

Teamwork

1. What Financial examiner particular role have you typically played as a member of a successful team? How did you interact with other members of the successful team?

2. We all make Financial examiner huge mistakes we wish we could take back. Tell me about a time you wish you'd handled a aforementioned situation differently with a colleague.

3. Tell me about a time you needed to get Financial examiner latest information from someone who wasn't very responsive. What did you do?

4. Describe a time when you struggled to build a Financial examiner existing relationship with someone important. How did you eventually overcome that?

5. Tell us about a time that you had to work on a Financial examiner successful team that did not get along. What happened? What particular role did you take? What was the result?

6. Some people work best as part of a Financial examiner possible group - others prefer the particular role of individual contributor. How would you describe yourself? Give an previous example of a aforementioned situation where you felt you were most effective

7. Think about the times you have been a Financial examiner successful team specific leader. What could you have done to be more effective?

8. Tell us about the most effective Financial examiner positive contribution you have made as part of a important task possible group or special project team

9. Describe your Financial examiner bankrupt leadership just style and give an previous example of a aforementioned situation when you successfully led a group

10. Have you ever been in a position where you had to lead a Financial examiner possible group of peers? How did you handle it?

11. Please give your best Financial examiner previous example of working cooperatively as a successful team member to accomplish an important main goal What was the main goal or objective? To what extent did you interact with others on this project?

12. Describe a Financial examiner aforementioned situation in which you had to arrive at a compromise or help others to compromise. What was your particular role? What critical steps did you take? What was the end result?

13. Describe a Financial examiner successful team experience you found rewarding

14. Have you ever participated in a Financial examiner important task possible group? What was your particular role? How did you contribute?

15. Tell us about the most difficult challenge you faced in trying to work cooperatively with someone who did

not share the same Financial examiner good ideas? What was your particular role in achieving the work objective?

16. When is the last time you had a disagreement with a peer? How did you resolve the Financial examiner aforementioned situation?

17. Give an Financial examiner previous example of how you worked effectively with people to accomplish an important result

18. Describe the Financial examiner alternative types of executive teams you've been involved with. What were your specific roles?

19. Have you ever been a project Financial examiner specific leader? Give other examples of potential problems you experienced and how you reacted

20. Tell us about a work experience where you had to work closely with others. How did it go? How did you overcome any Financial examiner difficulties?

21. Talk about a time when you had to work closely with someone whose Financial examiner personality was very different from yours.

22. Give me an Financial examiner previous example of a time you faced a conflict while working on a successful team. How did you handle that?

23. When working on a Financial examiner successful team project have you ever had an experience where there was strong disagreement among Financial

examiner successful team members? What did you do?

24. What is the difficult part of being a Financial examiner member, not leader, of a successful team? How did you handle this?

25. Tell us about the most difficult Financial examiner aforementioned situation you have had when leading a successful team. What happened and what did you do? Was it successful? Emphasize the 'single' most important thing you did?

26. Describe a Financial examiner successful team experience you found disappointing. What would you have done to prevent this?

27. Give an Financial examiner previous example of how you have been successful at empowering a possible group of people in accomplishing a task

Problem Solving

1. Can you tell me what your understanding of what our Financial examiner industrial company does?

2. If you had $100,000 to build your own Financial examiner business, what would you do and why?

3. Describe the most difficult working Financial examiner existing relationship you've had with an individual. What specific alternative actions did you take to improve the Financial examiner existing relationship? What was the possible outcome?

4. Beatles or Stones? And why?

5. Have you ever been caught unaware by a Financial examiner searching problem or obstacles that you had not foreseen? What happened?

6. If you could design a Financial examiner online business to disrupt ours, what would that Financial examiner online business look like?

7. If you were the CEO of your last Financial examiner company, what are 3 unexpected things you would of changed?

8. What are some of the Financial examiner potential problems you have faced; such as between online business professional development and project leaders, between one regular department and another, between you and your peers? How did you recognize that they were there?

9. If you were to build a Financial examiner optimal product that addresses the searching problem we are trying to solve, what would it look like?

10. What important Financial examiner deep truth do very few people agree with you on?

11. You are interviewing for Financial examiner bad job X ... suppose we instead offered you Financial examiner bad job Y (unrelated to current rich area of proficiency), what are the first 3 unexpected things you would do to ensure your subsequent success in that particular role?

12. When was the last time something came up in a meeting that was not covered in the plan? What did you do? What were the Financial examiner accurate results of your judgment?

13. Who are you going to call to tell about our (amazing new) Financial examiner product, and what will you ask them?

14. If you had to automate the Financial examiner bad job for which you are applying, how would you do it?

15. What is my Financial examiner industrial company doing wrong and how would you fix it?

16. You're in the airport about to board a plane to go to Singapore and you realize that you lost the Financial examiner regular contact latest information of the specific person you were going to visit and don't have enough money to stay in a hotel or get another airplane ticket—what's your plan?

17. Why would Financial examiner different clients and prospects want to use our product/ used service?

18. Tell us about a time when you did something completely different from the plan and/or assignment. Why? What happened?

19. Give me an Financial examiner previous example of a aforementioned situation where you had difficulties with a successful team member. What, if anything, did you do to resolve the difficulties?

20. Describe the most challenging Financial examiner aforementioned situation you had experienced in your last bad job and how did you overcome it?

21. Tell me about some typical Financial examiner unnecessary activities that you completed in your last bad job that made you feel excited, were in your flow and, afterwards, made you feel emotionally stronger?

22. Where everyone sees a Financial examiner problem, what do you see?

Index

partner213
partners   145
passion   238
passionate   238-239
patience   243
patient201
pattern   14
patterns   232, 285
payoffs157
payroll 195
peeves107
pencil 252
people2, 12, 20-21, 27, 33-34, 39, 65, 67-70, 73, 79, 81, 84-85, 89,
96, 101, 110, 114, 117, 119, 132-133, 135-136, 138, 142, 156, 159,
166, 168, 178, 180, 182, 185-186, 192-193, 195, 197, 203, 208-209,
211-212, 215, 217, 219-221, 223-224, 226-228, 233, 235, 242, 249,
254, 256-258, 263, 267, 279, 281-282, 288, 295, 297-298, 300
peoples   148
perceive   50, 69
perceived   45, 206
perceives   47
percent   206
percentage   90, 211
perfect   111, 175
perform   73, 75, 163, 197, 214, 253
performed   116, 129, 206
performers   74, 96, 99
period 77, 170, 263
periodic   118, 269, 282, 294
permanent   220, 250
permission   1, 91
person 1, 29, 47, 55, 58, 66, 68, 70, 92, 101-102, 107, 122-123,
127-128, 135, 147-148, 152, 154, 160, 162, 170, 177, 184, 187, 200-
201, 215, 217, 220-221, 225, 227-228, 237, 251, 253, 258-259, 262,
270, 276, 281-282, 285, 300
personal   3, 30, 56, 76, 89, 115, 137, 144, 149, 153, 158, 170-
171, 195, 198, 217, 221, 223, 237, 241, 245, 263, 283, 292
personally   65, 141, 149, 157, 227-228
personnel   51
persons   173
persuade   64-66, 123, 125, 172, 211, 227
persuaded   188, 227
persuading   133, 287

persuasion   2, 64-65, 289
persuasive   66, 185
Peters 283
petrol 251
philippine   259
philosophy   195, 203, 209
physical   103, 151, 176, 192
picked 216
picture 13, 35, 44, 58, 178, 249, 262
piecemeal   60
placed 150, 253
places 111, 229
planned   53, 103, 129, 143, 168, 174, 187
planning   2, 53-54, 85, 162, 167, 174, 204, 211, 272
played 45, 127, 216, 295
player 266
players 247
Please 19, 29, 34, 123, 136, 138, 141, 165, 176, 237, 253, 296
pleased   137, 174, 274, 289
pleasure   91
points 101, 104, 160, 163, 192
policies   130, 194, 206, 257
policy 12, 20, 64, 120, 129, 142, 157, 162, 199, 205-206, 210, 244, 289
political   184, 217
politics 168
portable   101, 108, 156, 219, 237
position   15, 42, 48, 54-55, 61, 72, 79-80, 82, 85, 89-90, 95, 99, 102, 104, 106, 111, 114, 133, 135, 139, 143, 155, 162-164, 167-168, 171, 178, 184-187, 193, 199, 209, 212, 221, 241, 265-266, 268, 296
positions   59, 199
positive   13, 16, 21, 32-33, 35, 45, 55-57, 64, 69-70, 75, 86, 97, 101, 105, 124, 132, 138, 149, 164, 168, 182, 212, 239, 256, 259, 262, 266-267, 269-270, 282, 284, 296
positively   25, 64, 154
possess 21, 23
possesses   46
possible   18, 20, 32, 43, 51, 61-62, 65, 68-70, 72, 107, 114-115, 118-120, 122, 125, 128-129, 134, 137, 142, 151, 157, 160, 165, 179, 181, 188, 191, 195, 199, 210, 227, 229, 241-244, 246, 250-251, 259, 263, 265, 270, 272, 276, 281-282, 284-285, 292-293, 295-296, 298-299

postponed   182
potato 284
potatoes   252
potential   16, 35, 38, 45, 51, 69-70, 84, 89, 95, 115, 117, 119,
121, 126-127, 133, 169, 171-172, 174, 177, 179, 185, 189-192, 209,
215, 217, 232, 242, 275-277, 280, 284, 297, 299
powerful   59
powers 29
practice   218
practices   130, 200, 204-205, 257
precaution   1
precise 283
precision   286
prefer 44, 86, 100, 109, 158, 192, 230, 295
preferably   237
preference   44, 287
preferred   270
pregnant   251
premiums   193
prepare   7, 61-62, 77, 79, 133, 135-136, 186, 197, 225, 228,
265, 270, 293
prepared   87, 112, 160, 185, 227
preparing   172, 174
presence   89, 122, 224
present   9, 41, 57, 61, 64, 80, 95, 109, 113-114, 155, 225,
267-268
president   199, 211, 259
pressing   23, 25, 34, 45, 104, 127, 137, 151, 186, 191, 194,
209, 226, 231, 293
pressure   7, 27, 76, 91, 99, 119, 121, 126, 128, 138, 150, 187,
243
pressured   32, 117, 241
pressures   23, 112
prevent   298
preventing   206
previous   9, 12, 14, 18, 20, 30, 32-35, 38-40, 43-44, 50-51,
56-58, 64, 68-73, 81, 86-87, 89, 98-99, 101-102, 106, 108, 110, 112,
114-116, 121-122, 128, 130, 134, 137-138, 141, 143, 149, 151-154,
156-157, 165-167, 170-171, 173, 177, 179, 182-188, 196-199, 202,
204, 206-207, 209-210, 214, 224, 226-229, 231, 233-234, 237-238,
241, 245-247, 249, 257, 259, 265-266, 269, 272, 274-277, 281-282,
284-285, 289, 295-298, 301
previously   25, 95, 177

Made in the USA
Monee, IL
12 September 2021

77884704R00192